Copy 27

# A FIRST THESAURUS

By Harriet Wittels
and
Joan Greisman

A GOLDEN BOOK • NEW YORK
Western Publishing Company, Inc.
Racine, Wisconsin 53404

*For Brad, Sherry, Mark, Adam, Craig, and Amy*

# Introduction

**Riddle:** What sounds like Brontosaurus, but is found on a bookshelf near the dictionaries, not at the natural history museum?

**Answer:** A thesaurus, of course! A thesaurus is a book that lists synonyms—words that have almost the same meaning; and antonyms—words of opposite meaning. **A First Thesaurus** will give you many accurate, interesting, and colorful new words to use, in addition to the old ones you already know. You will find this book useful, helpful, practical, handy, valuable, and beneficial. That is its aim, purpose, goal, object, and target.

# Using the Thesaurus

**Entry Words**

The words in **A First Thesaurus** that have synonyms and antonyms are called **entry words**. They are listed in alphabetical order, and printed in dark type:

    **bleak**   dreary, dismal   cheerful
    **blend**   mix, combine, join   separate
    **bless**   praise, thank, glorify   curse

Look in the "A" section. What entry word comes just before **accident**? (Answer: **accept**.) Now look in the "B's." What entry word comes right after **brand**? Look in the "C's." Between which two entry words do you find **car**?

**Guide Words**

The two words at the top of every page, in dark type, are called **guide words**. They are the first and last entry words on each page, and they will "guide" you to all the entry words between them.

Here's an example: If the guide words were **change** and **chop**, you would find the entry word **chest** on that page. But you would not find the entry word **climb** on that page. Now look up the entry word **decide**. What are the two guide words at the top of the page?

**Synonyms**

**Synonyms** are words that have the same, or almost the

4

same, meaning. Here are two groups of synonyms:

**embarrassed**   ashamed, humiliated, mortified
**embrace**   grasp, hug, hold, clutch

Synonyms can usually be substituted for one another in a sentence:

**fad**   style, fashion, craze, rage
Blue jeans are now the <u>fad</u>.
Blue jeans are now the <u>style</u>.
Blue jeans are now the <u>fashion</u>.
Blue jeans are now the <u>craze</u>.
Blue jeans are now the <u>rage</u>.

But sometimes synonyms cannot be substituted for one another in a sentence. Look at this group:

**match**   contest, game, battle
Today we had a spelling <u>match</u> in our class.
Today we had a spelling <u>contest</u> in our class.
Today we had a spelling <u>game</u> in our class.

But you wouldn't say:
Today we had a spelling <u>battle</u> in our class.

When you look up a word in this book, you may find that not all of the synonyms fit correctly in your sentence. You'll have to use common sense and good judgment in choosing the right word.

## Antonyms
A word that has the opposite meaning to that of the entry

word is called an **antonym**. You will find it in red, at the end of a group of synonyms:

**like** enjoy, admire, appreciate  dislike
**misty** cloudy, foggy, smoky  clear

Here's an example:

She doesn't like <u>short</u> hair, so she wears hers <u>long</u>.

The word "long" is the antonym of the word "short."

Now you try. Look up the entry word in dark type and find the antonyms to complete these sentences:

Cinderella was **beautiful**, but her stepsisters were

_____.

It takes longer to **pack** the car than to _____ it.

## Entry Words With More Than One Meaning

Some entry words, like **tag**, have more than one meaning. Tag could mean follow, shadow, trail, pursue, or tail. But tag could also mean label, name, or brand. That's why tag has two numbers for the two groups of synonyms. Here's another example:

**tape** 1. wrap, bind, tie
**tape** 2. record

In this book, the entry word **run** has five numbers for its five different meanings. Look up the entry word **run**, and in the following sentences, find the number of the correct group of synonyms.

The computer can only <u>run</u> on electricity. (Answer: 3.)
Will Tom <u>run</u> for class president this term? (?)
Susan had to <u>run</u> to catch the bus. (?)
Let the water <u>run</u> until it's cold. (?)
Our principal knows how to <u>run</u> our school. (?)

## Entry Words That Are Spelled the Same

Some entry words are spelled the same, but we say them differently and they have completely different meanings. That's why these words have different numbers in front of them. Look at the two entry words below and how they are used.

**1. minute**   instant, moment
**2. minute**   tiny, small, miniature   giant
Billy's dog runs to him the <u>minute</u> he whistles. (**1.**)
You must use a microscope to see those <u>minute</u>
germs. (**2.**)

Now see if you can complete the sentences below with the correct entry word and its number.

**1. close**   shut, fasten, lock   open
**2. close**   near, approaching   far
School children love the month of June, because
summer vacation is _____.
Please _____ the door behind you.

That's how **A First Thesaurus** works. It's easy and fun. Use it often. Make it a habit and you'll find that it will help to improve your reading, your writing, and your speech.

# A

**abandon**   desert, forsake, leave
**ability**   skill, talent, know-how   inability
**abnormal**   odd, unnatural, irregular   normal
**about**   1. almost, nearly, approximately, around
**about**   2. concerning, of
**abrupt**   sudden, unexpected   expected
**absent**   away, truant   present
**absorb**   take in, soak up, sponge
**absurd**   unbelievable, ridiculous, ludicrous   sensible
**abuse**   mistreat, damage
**accept**   adopt, believe, approve, consent to   deny
**accident**   mishap, fluke
**accomplish**   complete, do, carry out, finish, achieve
**account**   story, reason, description, statement
**accumulate**   collect, assemble, gather, compile,
   store up
**accurate**   correct, right, perfect   inaccurate, wrong
**accuse**   blame, charge

actor

**ache** pain, throb, hurt

**achieve** accomplish, fulfill

**act** perform, behave

**active** lively, peppy, spirited, energetic inactive, lazy

**actor** performer, entertainer

**actual** real, true, genuine, authentic

**add** put together, join subtract

**adequate** enough, sufficient, satisfactory insufficient

**admire** like, respect, appreciate

**admit** 1. confess, acknowledge deny

**admit** 2. allow to enter, receive

**adore** love, worship, idolize, cherish, revere hate

**adult** grown-up, mature immature, juvenile

**advance** proceed, progress, further recede

**advertise** announce, publicize, promote

**advise** suggest, recommend, direct, counsel

**affair** 1. happening, occasion, occurrence, event, party, festivity

**affair** 2. business, concern, interest

**affection** liking, fondness dislike

**afraid** frightened, scared, alarmed unafraid, fearless

**again** once more, another time

**agony**   suffering, pain, distress, torture

**agree**   consent to, comply with, approve of   disagree, differ with

**agreement**   pact, contract, treaty, bargain, deal, understanding

**aid**   help, assist, support, serve   hinder

**aim**   purpose, goal, object, target

**alarm**   scare, frighten, startle, shock, unnerve   calm, soothe

**alert**   wide-awake, watchful, ready   dull

**alibi**   excuse, story

**allow**   permit, let   forbid, deny

**allowance**   allotment, grant, budget

**almost**   about, nearly, approximately, practically

**alone**   solitary, isolated, sole

**also**   too, in addition, besides, as well

**always**   forever, for good, for keeps   never

**amend**   change, correct, improve

**among**   surrounded by, amid, in with

**amount**   sum, quantity

**amusing**   funny, entertaining, delightful, comical, humorous   boring, dull

**anchor**   1. fasten, fix, secure, attach

**anchor**   2. ship hook

anchor (2)

**ancient**   old, aged, antique   modern, new

**angry**   furious, enraged, annoyed, cross

**animal**   beast, creature

**announce**   state, broadcast, proclaim, make known

**annoy**   bother, disturb, tease, irritate, anger, pester, provoke

**answer**   reply, response   question

**apparel**   clothing, dress, garments, attire

**appear**   1. seem, look

**appear**   2. arrive, approach, enter

**appliance**   tool, device, instrument, implement, utensil, gadget

**appoint**   choose, name, assign, nominate

**appreciate**   enjoy, value, respect, admire

**appropriate**   suitable, fitting, proper   inappropriate, unsuitable

**approximately**   nearly, closely, roughly, about   exactly

**area**   region, district, section, location, territory, zone

**argue**   disagree, quarrel, squabble, bicker   agree

**arid**   dry, waterless, parched   wet

**arm**   equip, fortify, empower   disarm

**army**   troops, forces, military

**aroma**   odor, fragrance, scent

**arrange**  organize, put in order, classify, sort

**arrest**  stop, seize, apprehend, capture

**arrive**  come, reach, get to, show up  go

**article**  1. story, essay, report

**article**  2. item, thing, object

**ashamed**  embarrassed, humiliated, mortified  proud

**ask**  request, question, inquire  answer

**assassinate**  kill, murder

**assault**  attack, offense, onslaught

**assemble**  1. meet, gather together, congregate  scatter

**assemble**  2. put together, set up, construct, build  demolish, take apart

**assignment**  task, chore, job, duty

**assist**  help, aid, support, lend a hand  hinder

**assorted**  various, several, different, mixed

**astonishing**  surprising, astounding, amazing

**athletic**  sporting, gymnastic

**attach**  fasten, join, connect, add  detach

**attack**  charge, bombard, ambush, storm, invade, raid

**attempt**  try, undertake, endeavor, strive

**attend**  go to, be present

**attention**  care, consideration, concern, thoughtfulness

award

**attract**  pull, interest, draw, lure  repel

**attractive**  lovely, pleasing, pretty, handsome
  unattractive, plain

**author**  writer

**autograph**  signature

**average**  ordinary, usual, common  unusual

**award**  prize, reward

**awful**  terrible, horrible, dreadful, atrocious  pleasant

**awkward**  clumsy, ungraceful, cumbersome, ungainly
  graceful

# B

bald

**baby**  infant, toddler

**bad**  evil, naughty  good

**balance**  equalize, stabilize, steady

**bald**  hairless, bare  hairy

**band**  orchestra

**bandit**  robber, thief, gangster, highwayman, outlaw

**bar**  1. shut out, ban, block, exclude  allow

**bar**  2. saloon, tavern

14

**bare**  uncovered, naked  covered

**barely**  scarcely, hardly

**barter**  trade, exchange, swap

**bashful**  shy, timid, modest, coy  bold

**basic**  fundamental, essential

**bat**  strike, hit, club

**battle**  fight, feud, war, struggle, combat, conflict

**bawl**  cry, weep

**beach**  shore, coast, seaside

**beam**  shine, glow

**beast**  animal, creature

**beat**  1. strike, hit, thrash, pound, pummel

**beat**  2. outdo, defeat, surpass, trounce

**beautiful**  attractive, lovely, pretty, handsome  ugly

**before**  earlier, previously, prior, formerly  after

**beg**  plead, implore

**begin**  start, commence, launch  end, conclude

**behind**  after, later than  ahead

**believe**  1. think, suppose, imagine, consider

**believe**  2. accept, trust  doubt

**belly**  stomach, abdomen

**beneath**  under, below  above

**beneficial**  helpful, useful, advantageous  harmful

**bet**   wager, gamble

**between**   among, betwixt

**beyond**   farther, past

**big**   1. large, huge, tremendous, enormous, immense
small

**big**   2. important, great, grand, considerable
unimportant

**birth**   beginning, origin, infancy   death, end

**bitter**   distasteful, unpleasant   pleasant, sweet

blade

**blade**   sword, knife

**blame**   accuse, charge, indict

**blank**   empty, vacant   filled

**blast**   explosion, blowout

**bleak**   dreary, dismal   cheerful

**blend**   mix, combine, join   separate

**bless**   praise, thank, glorify   curse

**blind**   sightless

**blizzard**   snowstorm

**block**   obstruct, hinder, check, restrain   permit

**blockade**   barrier, obstruction, barricade

**bluff**   deceive, trick, delude

**board**   mount, get on, embark   dismount, get off

**boisterous**   noisy, rowdy, shrill   quiet

16

**bold**  1. brave, courageous, fearless, gallant, heroic cowardly

**bold**  2. arrogant, brazen, defiant, insolent  timid

**bolt**  1. run, flee, break away

**bolt**  2. lock, fastener

**boring**  dull, uninteresting  interesting

**boss**  1. supervise, oversee, direct

**boss**  2. manager, foreman, employer

**bother**  annoy, pester, disturb, irritate, harass, provoke

**bottom**  base, foundation, lowest part  top

**bound**  enclosed, surrounded

**boundary**  limit, border

**box**  1. fight, hit

**box**  2. crate, container

box (2)

**brace**  support, prop

**brag**  boast, crow, gloat

**brake**  stop, slow down, decelerate, curb  accelerate

**branch**  shoot, bough, limb

**brand**  kind, sort, type

**brave**  bold, courageous, fearless, gallant, heroic cowardly

**brawl**  riot, racket, fracas

branch

**break**  1. fracture, crack, crush, split, smash, shatter mend, fix

17

**break**   2. interruption, interval, intermission, pause, recess, rest

**brief**   short, concise, terse   long

**bright**   1. cheerful, sunny, shiny, vivid, sparkling, gleaming, glowing   dull, dim

**bright**   2. smart, alert, intelligent   dull

**brilliant**   intelligent, wise   stupid

**bring**   carry, take, transport, deliver

**broad**   wide, expansive   narrow

**bruise**   wound, injure, hurt

**buddy**   friend, pal, companion, chum, partner

**build**   make, create, construct, establish, form demolish

**bulky**   broad, thick, lumpy   narrow

**bulletin**   message, newsletter

**bumpy**   uneven, rocky, coarse   smooth

**bundle**   parcel, package

**burglar**   thief, robber, housebreaker

burning

**burning**   hot, fiery, sizzling, blazing, flaming

**bury**   conceal, cover   uncover

**business**   work, occupation, profession, job

**busy**   active, occupied, engaged   idle

**button**   fasten, clasp, close   unbutton, open

**buy**   purchase, shop   sell

18

**by**   near, beside, at

# C

**cable**   telegraph, wire

**cafeteria**   restaurant, snack bar, cafe

**calculate**   compute, count, figure, estimate

**call**   1. shout, yell

**call**   2. telephone

**calm**   quiet, still, peaceful, serene, tranquil

**camouflage**   disguise

**campaign**   crusade, movement, cause, drive

**can**   container, tin, receptacle

can

**cancel**   erase, wipe out, repeal

**candidate**   applicant, nominee

**cap**   top, cover, crown

**capture**   seize, arrest, catch, trap, apprehend   free, release

**car**   automobile, vehicle

**care**   1. thought, worry, attention, concern   neglect

**care**   2. protection, supervision, custody

**careful**   cautious, watchful   careless

19

carpet

**careless** sloppy, reckless, thoughtless careful
**carnival** fair, festival
**carpet** rug, mat
**carry** hold, transport, tote
**carve** cut, slice
**catalog** list, classify, group, sort
**catastrophe** tragedy, disaster, calamity
**catch** capture, seize, trap release, free
**cautious** careful, watchful, thoughtful careless
**cease** stop, end, halt, quit, conclude, discontinue
continue
**celebrate** 1. proclaim, observe, commemorate
**celebrate** 2. rejoice
**cemetery** graveyard
**center** middle, heart, hub, core, nucleus
**certain** sure, positive, definite unsure

chair

**chair** seat, bench
**challenge** dare, defy, confront
**champion** winner, victor, best
**chance** 1. opportunity, occasion
**chance** 2. possibility, likelihood, prospect
**chance** 3. fate, luck
**change** alter, modify, vary, switch maintain
**chapter** section, part, division

20

**character**  1. nature, temperament, makeup, disposition

**character**  2. role, part

**charming**  appealing, pleasing, delightful  unpleasant

**chase**  1. follow, run after, pursue

**chase**  2. drive away, repulse, reject

**chat**  talk, gossip, discuss, converse

**cheap**  inexpensive, low-priced  expensive

**cheat**  trick, deceive, swindle, defraud, dupe, bamboozle, mislead

**check**  1. restrain, curb, stop, control

**check**  2. prove, mark, verify

**cheerful**  happy, glad, joyful, jolly, gay, merry  sad, downcast

**chest**  box, locker, safe

**child**  youngster, kid  adult

**chilly**  cool, brisk, nippy  warm

**chisel**  sculpture, carve

**choke**  strangle, suffocate, smother

**choose**  pick, select, elect, opt

**chop**  cut, cleave, sever, hack

**chore**  task, job, work, assignment

**chubby**  plump, fat, stout, stocky  skinny

chubby

**chuckle**   giggle, laugh, titter

**chum**   friend, pal, companion, partner

**city**   metropolis, municipality

**clamor**   racket, ruckus, din, uproar, commotion
   stillness, quiet

**clean**   spotless, spick-and-span   dirty

**clear**   1. remove, eliminate, rid

**clear**   2. bright, shining, vivid   muddy, dull

**clever**   smart, alert, bright, skillful, wise, sharp,
   intelligent, quick-witted   dull

**client**   customer, patron

**climate**   weather

**climb**   mount, rise, ascend   descend

**clip**   1. cut, shear, crop, snip

**clip**   2. fasten, attach

**1. close**   1. shut, fasten, lock   open

   **close**   2. end, finish, complete, conclude, stop   start

**2. close**   near, approaching   far

**cloudy**   dark, overcast, dismal   clear

**club**   1. group, association, clique

club (2)   **club**   2. bat, stick

**club**   3. strike, hit, knock

**clue**   sign, hint, evidence, lead

**clumsy** awkward, ungraceful, ungainly, gawky graceful

**coach** train, tutor, teach

**coarse** 1. rough, uneven, bumpy, rocky, ragged smooth

**coarse** 2. crude, vulgar, common refined

**code** laws, rules

**cold** chilly, frosty hot

**collapse** fall, topple

**collect** gather, accumulate, assemble scatter

**colossal** huge, gigantic, vast, immense, enormous, mammoth tiny

**combine** join, unite, mix, blend, merge separate

**comedian** comic, funnyman

**comfortable** satisfied, contented, cozy, snug uncomfortable

**comical** amusing, entertaining, funny, humorous, witty

**command** order, direct, instruct

**committee** group, council, delegation

**common** 1. regular, ordinary, usual, familiar, everyday unusual, odd

**common** 2. coarse, crude, vulgar refined

**commotion** racket, ruckus, disturbance, tumult, confusion, fuss, excitement, clamor, hubbub, to-do order, calmness

**communicate**  inform, tell, enlighten

**community**  district, area, town

**companion**  friend, pal, chum, partner

**company**  1. business, firm, enterprise

**company**  2. guests, visitors

**compare**  match, liken, contrast

**complete**  1. end, finish, conclude, wind up  start

**complete**  2. whole, entire  incomplete

**complicated**  hard, involved, difficult, complex
  simple

**compliment**  praise, commend, flatter

**conceal**  hide, cover, mask, camouflage  disclose,
  reveal

**conceited**  vain, boastful, cocky, egotistical  modest

**concern**  1. interest, care, worry

**concern**  2. business, company, firm

**concert**  musical performance, recital

**conclude**  end, finish, complete, close, stop  open,
  begin

**condition**  circumstance, situation, state

**1. conduct**  manage, direct, lead, guide

**2. conduct**  behavior, manner

**confident**  certain, sure, convinced, self-reliant
  doubtful

24

**confuse**  complicate, bewilder, dumfound, muddle, baffle, perplex, puzzle  clarify

**congratulate**  compliment, commend, praise

**connect**  join, unite, combine, link, attach  separate, disconnect

**conquer**  overcome, overwhelm, overtake, overthrow, defeat, crush

**consent**  permission, approval, acceptance, agreement  refusal

**conserve**  keep, save, preserve  waste

**consider**  think, study, ponder, contemplate, imagine

**considerate**  thoughtful, kind, sympathetic, tactful  inconsiderate, unkind

**console**  comfort, reassure, soothe

**constantly**  continually, always

**construct**  make, manufacture, build, form, create, assemble  demolish

**consume**  eat, devour

**contain**  hold, include, consist of, comprise

**contented**  satisfied, pleased  discontented, dissatisfied

**contest**  game, tournament, competition

**continue**  persist, go on, keep on  discontinue, stop

**control**  restrain, check, curb

**convenient**  easy, handy, suitable  inconvenient

25

**conversation**  talk, chat, discussion

**convert**  change, transform

**convict**  condemn, sentence  clear, acquit

**convince**  persuade

**cool**  1. chilly  warm

**cool**  2. calm, unexcited  excited

**cooperate**  support, help, work together, collaborate  hinder

**copy**  imitate, duplicate, echo, repeat, reproduce

**correct**  1. right, true, accurate, proper, exact, appropriate  incorrect, wrong

**correct**  2. improve, remedy

**correspond**  write, communicate with

**corridor**  hallway, passageway, aisle

**counterfeit**  fake, imitation, copied  real

**country**  nation, land

**courageous**  brave, bold, fearless, gallant, heroic  cowardly

**course**  line, track, direction

**courteous**  polite, respectful, civil, gracious  rude

**cover**  1. hide, conceal, protect, shelter  uncover

**cover**  2. include, contain, consist of, comprise

**cowardly**  timid, weak  brave

**coy**  timid, shy, modest, bashful  **bold**

**crack**   break, split, fracture

**crammed**   stuffed, full, heaping, overflowing, loaded, packed, crowded, jammed

**cranky**   cross, annoyed, irritable, grouchy, disagreeable
pleasant

**crazy**   insane, mad, daft   sane

**create**   make, invent, originate, shape, form, manufacture, produce, design, establish

**crew**   team, gang, staff, force

**crime**   wrongdoing, sin, vice, evil

**crook**   criminal, gangster, lawbreaker

**cross**   cranky, annoyed, irritable, grouchy, disagreeable   pleasant

**crowd**   mob, throng, horde

**cruel**   mean, unkind, heartless, brutal, ruthless   kind

**crush**   press, squeeze, compress, squash

**cry**   weep, wail, sob, bawl

**cuddle**   snuggle, nestle

**cure**   heal, remedy

**curious**   inquisitive, nosy, prying, snoopy
uninterested

**current**   1. up-to-date, present, prevalent, new
old-fashioned

**current**   2. flow, stream

**curse**   swear, condemn

cry

27

**curve**  bend, wind, twist, turn

**custom**  way, manner, tradition, habit, practice

**customer**  client, buyer, patron

**cut**  1. snip, clip, slit, slash, saw, sever

**cut**  2. shorten, reduce, abbreviate, condense, abridge
  increase

**cute**  attractive, bright, pretty  unattractive

# D

**dainty**  delicate, fine, small  gross

**damage**  harm, hurt, impair, spoil  mend, fix

**damp**  moist, wet  dry

**dangerous**  unsafe, risky, hazardous  safe

**daring**  brave, bold, courageous, fearless, heroic
  afraid, timid

**dark**  dim, gloomy, dismal, somber, dreary  bright

**dart**  dash, rush, hurry, scurry  dawdle

**dash**  dart, rush, hurry, scurry  dawdle

**data**  facts, information

**date**  appointment, engagement

**dawdle**   idle, loiter, linger, delay, tarry   hurry

**dawn**   daybreak, sunrise   dusk

**dazzling**   brilliant, shiny, glowing, glistening, blinding   dull

**dead**   lifeless, deceased, gone   alive

**deal**   agreement, understanding, bargain, transaction

**debate**   argue, dispute

**deceive**   cheat, trick, swindle, defraud, dupe, bamboozle, mislead

**decent**   proper, correct, suitable   improper

**decide**   settle, determine, resolve, judge

**declare**   say, state, exclaim, announce

**decorate**   beautify, trim, adorn

decorate

**decrease**   reduce, lessen, diminish, cut, shorten   increase

**deduct**   subtract, remove, withdraw   add

**defeat**   overcome, triumph, outdo, surpass

**defend**   protect, safeguard, shield, support   attack

**define**   explain, describe, clarify

**definite**   clear, precise, clear-cut, exact   unclear

**deform**   spoil, disfigure, mar

**delay**   postpone, put off, detain, stall

**deliberately**   purposely, intentionally, knowingly   accidentally

**delicate**  mild, fine, dainty, fragile  gross

**delicious**  luscious, tasty, appetizing  tasteless

**delighted**  happy, jubilant, overjoyed, elated  unhappy

**delightful**  pleasant, lovely, charming, appealing, pleasing  unpleasant

**deliver**  hand over, transfer

**demand**  ask, request

**demolish**  wreck, destroy, dismantle  restore

**demon**  devil, fiend, monster, ogre

**demonstrate**  show, display, present, exhibit, illustrate

depart

**depart**  leave, exit  arrive

**dependable**  trustworthy, reliable  undependable

**deposit**  place, put, leave  withdraw

**depressed**  sad, dejected, discouraged, downhearted, blue  happy

**deprived**  wanting, lacking, needing, missing, without

**describe**  define, portray, depict, characterize

**desert**  leave, forsake, abandon

**deserve**  earn, merit

**design**  draw, plan, sketch

**desire**  wish, want, long for

**despise**  hate, loathe, detest  love

**destination**  goal, end, objective

**destroy**  spoil, ruin, wreck  restore

**detach**  separate, unfasten, disconnect  attach

**detest**  despise, hate, loathe  love

**detour**  by-pass

detour

**develop**  grow, mature, progress, advance, flourish

**devil**  demon, fiend, ogre, monster

**devotion**  1. love, affection, fondness

**devotion**  2. loyalty, dedication

**devour**  eat, consume

**diagram**  drawing, sketch, design

**diary**  account, record

**die**  pass away, perish, expire  live

**different**  unlike, distinct  same

diary

**difficult**  hard, complicated, troublesome  easy

**dig**  scoop, excavate

**dignified**  noble, majestic, grand, distinguished
undignified

**dim**  dull, dark, faint, weak, indistinct  bright

**dimension**  measurement, size, proportions

**dingy**  dirty, dull, dark  bright

**direct**  1. show, point out, guide, lead, steer, escort

**direct**  2. manage, control, conduct, lead, head, guide,
command

dig

31

dirty

**dirty**   soiled, filthy   clean

**disadvantage**   drawback, handicap   advantage

**disagree**   differ, quarrel, dispute, argue, oppose
  agree

**disappear**   vanish, fade away   appear

**disaster**   tragedy, calamity, misfortune, catastrophe

**discard**   throw away, reject, scrap   keep

**discharge**   dismiss, release, unload, dump

**discipline**   punish, correct, chastise

**discouraged**   depressed, dejected, downhearted
  encouraged

**discover**   find, uncover, reveal, unearth

**discuss**   talk over

**disease**   sickness, illness, ailment, malady

**disgrace**   shame, embarrassment

**disguise**   conceal, mask, camouflage   reveal

**disgusted**   sickened, offended, nauseated, revolted

**dishonest**   untruthful, deceitful, crooked, untrust-
  worthy   honest

**dismal**   dark, gloomy, dreary, bleak, depressing
  bright

**dismiss**   discharge, expel, release

**display**   show, present, exhibit, demonstrate

**dispute**   argue, quarrel, fight   agree

**distinct**   plain, clear, obvious, exact, definite, clear-cut
unclear

**distinguished**   famous, honored, outstanding, celebrated, dignified

**distribute**   dispense, allot, disperse   collect

**district**   area, region, section, neighborhood, zone

**disturb**   upset, annoy, bother

**divide**   separate, split   unite

**divorce**   separate, split   marry

**dizzy**   unsteady, confused, spinning   steady

**dock**   anchor, moor

dock

**doctor**   physician, medic

**document**   certificate, statement

**dodge**   duck, avoid, evade

**donate**   contribute, give, present, grant

**done**   complete, finished, ended, concluded
unfinished

**donkey**   burro, ass

**dose**   portion, amount, quantity

**doubt**   question, mistrust, suspect   believe, trust

**downfall**   defeat, failure, ruin

donkey

**downpour**   rainstorm, cloudburst, flood

**drab**   dull, lifeless, flat, unattractive   bright,
attractive

**draft**   1. wind, air current

**draft**   2. enlistment, enrollment, call-up, recruitment, induction

**drag**   pull, tug, draw, haul, tow

**drain**   empty, extract, draw off, remove   fill

**dramatize**   produce, present, stage

**draw**   1. sketch, portray, picture

**draw**   2. attract, lure   repel

**dreadful**   awful, terrible, horrible, vile, ghastly, wretched   wonderful

**dream**   imagine, fantasize

**dreary**   gloomy, dull, dismal, dim, dark   bright

**drench**   soak, wet, flood, saturate

dress

**dress**   clothe, outfit, attire

**drill**   practice, teach, train, exercise

**drive**   steer, handle, operate

**drizzle**   rain, shower, sprinkle

**droop**   sag, drag, hang, dangle

**drop**   end, cease, stop, let go, give up   start, continue

**drown**   sink, submerge, immerse

**drowsy**   sleepy, dreamy   alert

**drug**   medicine, narcotic

**drunk**   intoxicated, inebriated, tipsy   sober

**dry**   arid, parched   wet

**duck**   dodge, avoid, evade

**dull**   1. dim, dark, faint, weak, indistinct   bright

**dull**   2. stupid, slow, dim-witted, dumb   smart

**dull**   3. boring, uninteresting, monotonous   interesting

**dumb**   1. stupid, dull, dim-witted   smart

**dumb**   2. speechless, mute, silent

**dummy**   1. imitation, copy, model

**dummy**   2. dope, dolt, dunce, fool

**dump**   empty, unload, discard, scrap, throw away   load

**dunce**   dummy, dope, dolt, fool

**duplicate**   copy, repeat, reproduce, double

**dusk**   sunset, sundown, evening, nightfall   dawn

**duty**   task, job, chore, work, assignment, obligation, responsibility

**dye**   color, stain, tint

**dynamic**   active, energetic, forceful, intense   weak


# E

**eager**   anxious, enthusiastic

**earn**   deserve, merit, gain

earth (2)

**earth**  1. soil, dirt, ground

**earth**  2. world, globe

**easy**  simple, plain, uncomplicated  hard

**eat**  dine, consume

**echo**  reflect, resound, reverberate

**eclipse**  blackout, shadow

**edge**  border, frame, rim

**edit**  correct, check, rewrite, revise, amend

**educate**  teach, train, tutor, instruct, enlighten

**eerie**  weird, spooky, strange, ghostly

**effort**  try, attempt, undertaking, endeavor

**elastic**  flexible, springy, stretchable  inflexible

**elder**  older, senior  younger

**elect**  pick, select, choose

**elegant**  refined, tasteful, polished  common, vulgar

**elementary**  basic, beginning, introductory, fundamental, primary  advanced

**elevate**  lift, raise, boost, hoist  lower

**eligible**  qualified, fit, suitable  ineligible

**eliminate**  discard, remove, throw out, reject, exclude
include

**else**  other, different

**embarrassed**  ashamed, humiliated, mortified

**embrace**  grasp, hug, hold, clutch

**emergency**  crisis, pinch

**emotion**   feeling, sentiment

**emphasize**   stress, accent, highlight

**employ**   hire, sign up, engage   fire

**empty**   blank, vacant, hollow, barren   full

**enclosed**   surrounded, fenced, contained, restricted, encircled   open

**encourage**   urge, nudge, prod, support, inspire   discourage

**end**   finish, stop, cease, complete, conclude, terminate, discontinue, quit   begin

**endless**   constant, continuous, nonstop, infinite

**enemy**   foe, opponent, opposition   friend

**energy**   strength, force, power, might, vitality, pep, vigor

**engrave**   print, inscribe, stamp, carve

**enjoy**   like, admire, relish   dislike

**enlarge**   expand, inflate, increase, amplify, magnify   reduce, shrink

**enlist**   enroll, register, sign up, join

**enormous**   huge, giant, immense, vast, gigantic, colossal   tiny

**enough**   plenty, sufficient, ample, adequate   insufficient

**enraged**   angry, mad, furious, provoked

**enroll**   enlist, register, join, sign up

**entertaining**   interesting, amusing, fascinating, absorbing, delightful   boring, dull

**enthusiastic**  eager, interested  indifferent

**entire**  whole, full, complete, total  partial

**envious**  jealous

**environment**  neighborhood, surroundings

**equal**  tie, match, parallel

**equip**  provide, furnish, supply, outfit

**erase**  rub out, cancel

**erect**  build, construct

**errand**  task, job, assignment, chore

**escape**  flee, get away

**escort**  accompany, chaperone

**essay**  composition, article, paper

**essential**  important, needed, necessary, vital
  unimportant

**establish**  create, set up, organize, form

**estimate**  figure, judge, guess, compute, calculate

**etiquette**  manners, rules of conduct, amenities

**evaporate**  fade away, disappear, vanish

**even**  1. level, flat, smooth  uneven

**even**  2. same, equal, identical  different

**evening**  sunset, sundown, dusk, nightfall  morning

**event**  incident, happening, experience, occurrence

**eventually**  finally, in time, ultimately

**evict**  expel, oust, turn out

**evidence**   facts, proof, signs, clues

**evil**   bad, sinful, wicked   good

**exactly**   precisely

**exaggerate**   magnify, stretch, overstate   minimize

**examine**   1. inspect, study, observe

**examine**   2. test, quiz, question

**example**   sample, model, specimen

**excellent**   very good, fine, splendid, superb   inferior

**except**   excluding, besides, barring   including

**exceptional**   notable, outstanding, unusual, extraordinary, remarkable   ordinary

**exchange**   trade, change, substitute, switch, swap

**excited**   enthusiastic, eager, interested   indifferent

**excursion**   trip, journey, tour, outing

**1. excuse**   reason, alibi

**2. excuse**   pardon, forgive, absolve   blame

**executive**   administrator, manager, director, officer

**exercise**   practice, drill, train, prepare, condition

**exhausted**   tired, weary, fatigued   energetic

**exhibit**   show, display, present, demonstrate

**exile**   banish, expel, deport

**exit**   depart, go out, leave   enter

**expand**   spread, grow, enlarge, increase, broaden   contract, reduce

exercise

**expect**   look for, await, anticipate

**expedition**   journey, trip, pilgrimage

**expel**   remove, discharge, dismiss, oust   admit

**expensive**   costly, high-priced, dear   cheap

**experience**   event, incident, happening, occurrence

**experiment**   try, test

**expired**   ended, ceased, discontinued

**explain**   clarify, describe, simplify

**explode**   burst, blow up

**explore**   search, research, investigate, probe

**express**   1. fast, quick, speedy, rapid, swift   slow

**express**   2. present, tell, describe

**exquisite**   beautiful, gorgeous, stunning, dazzling
  ugly

**extend**   increase, enlarge, stretch, lengthen, expand,
  broaden   reduce, decrease

**exterminate**   destroy, get rid of, eliminate, kill,
  wipe out

**extinct**   dead, gone, obsolete

**extinguish**   put out, smother, crush

**extra**   additional, more, spare, surplus

**extraordinary**   special, unusual, remarkable, exceptional, noteworthy, memorable   ordinary

**extreme**   exaggerated, overdone, extravagant
  moderate

# F

**fable**  story, fairy tale, legend, myth

**fabric**  cloth, material

**fabulous**  wonderful, marvelous, splendid, superb, spectacular, remarkable

**face**  meet, confront, encounter

**fact**  detail, item, point

**factory**  plant

**fad**  style, fashion, craze, rage

**fade**  dim, lose color, weaken

**fail**  flop, flunk, be unsuccessful   succeed

**faint**  1. weak, dim, faded, pale, dull, hazy   strong, bright

**faint**  2. black out, swoon, weaken

**fair**  1. right, correct, just, honest, impartial   unfair, unjust

**fair**  2. sunny, clear, pleasant, bright   cloudy

**fair**  3. average, mediocre

**fair**  4. light, pale   dark

**fair**  5. festival, bazaar

fabric

41

fall (1)

**fairy**   elf, pixie, sprite

**faith**   1. trust, hope, belief, confidence

**faith**   2. religion, teaching

**fake**   imitation, false, counterfeit   real

**fall**   1. drop, descend, tumble, topple, plunge, collapse   rise

**fall**   2. autumn

**false**   1. wrong, incorrect, untrue   true

**false**   2. fake, counterfeit   real

**familiar**   popular, well-known, common   strange

**family**   group, kin, relatives, folks

**famous**   popular, well-known, celebrated, renowned

**fan**   admirer, follower

**fancy**   elaborate, frilly, flowery, fussy, ornate   simple, plain

**fantastic**   incredible, unusual, extraordinary, exceptional, remarkable, wonderful, marvelous   ordinary

**far**   distant, remote, removed   near

**fare**   charge, toll, fee

**farm**   grow, raise, harvest, cultivate

**fascinating**   interesting, absorbing, exciting, thrilling, captivating   boring

**fashion**   1. make, form, shape, create, mold

**fashion**   2. style, mode, vogue

**fast**   rapid, swift, speedy, quick   slow

farm

**fasten**   secure, tie, bind, attach, close, seal   untie, open

**fat**   heavy, stout, plump, chubby   thin

**faucet**   spigot, tap

**fault**   mistake, error

**favor**   good deed, kindness, service

**favorite**   best, choice, prized, pet

**fear**   fright, dread, alarm, panic, terror

**fearless**   brave, daring, bold, courageous, heroic   afraid

**feast**   banquet, treat

**fee**   charge, fare, toll, dues

**feeble**   weak, frail   strong

**feed**   nourish, supply, nurture

**feel**   touch, handle, finger

**female**   feminine, womanly   male

**fence**   1. enclosure, wall, barrier

**fence**   2. fight, duel, joust

**ferocious**   fierce, savage, vicious, brutal, cruel, wild, ruthless   tame

**fertile**   fruitful, rich, productive   barren

**feud**   fight, disagree, argue, dispute, quarrel, battle

**fib**   lie, untruth, falsehood

**field**   land, tract, plot

**fiend**   devil, demon, monster, ogre

**fierce** ferocious, violent, raging, savage, wild, vicious
gentle

**fiery** hot, burning, flaming

**fight** dispute, feud, battle, struggle

**figure** shape, form, build, physique

**file** 1. sort, classify, group, categorize

**file** 2. grind, smooth, sand, sharpen

**fill** load, pack, stuff, supply empty

**filter** strain, screen, sift, separate

**filthy** dirty, grimy, polluted clean

**final** last, closing, concluding beginning

**finale** end, conclusion, finish opening

**find** discover, detect, learn, uncover, disclose lose

**fine** 1. good, excellent, splendid

**fine** 2. delicate, dainty rough

**fine** 3. penalize, charge, tax

**finish** end, conclude, complete, close, stop start

**fire** 1. blaze, flame

**fire** 2. dismiss, discharge, lay off hire

**fire** 3. shoot, discharge, blast

**firm** 1. hard, solid, rigid, inflexible, immovable
flexible

**firm** 2. company, business, enterprise

**fit** 1. healthy, strong, well unfit

**fit** 2. attack, seizure, spell, convulsion

**fix**   repair, mend, adjust, regulate   break

**flag**   pennant, banner, standard

**flame**   fire, blaze

**flat**   smooth, even, level   uneven

**flatter**   praise, compliment

**flee**   run away, bolt, escape

**flexible**   elastic, springy, stretchable, pliable   rigid, inflexible

**flimsy**   weak, fragile   strong, sturdy

**fling**   toss, hurl, pitch, throw

**flood**   overfill, drench, overflow

**floor**   1. ground, pavement

**floor**   2. level, story

**flower**   blossom, bloom, develop, flourish

**fluid**   liquid, flowing, watery   solid

**fly**   soar, glide

**foe**   enemy, opponent   friend

**foggy**   cloudy, dim, smoky, misty   clear

**fold**   bend, double over, crease   unfold

**follow**   1. chase, trail, track, pursue

**follow**   2. obey, use, practice

**fondness**   liking, love, affection

**foolish**   silly, stupid, dumb, ridiculous, senseless

**forbid**   prohibit, bar, ban, prevent   allow

flag

fling

**45**

**force**   1. compel, make, drive, pressure, push

**force**   2. power, strength, energy

**forecast**   prediction, prophecy

**forgive**   pardon, excuse, absolve   blame

**forlorn**   sad, hopeless, melancholy, unhappy, downcast, despondent   cheerful

**form**   make, develop, shape, fashion, create, construct, mold

**fortunate**   lucky   unlucky

**forward**   onward, ahead   backward

**foundation**   1. base, ground

**foundation**   2. establishment, organization, institution

**fraction**   part, portion, segment

**fracture**   break, crack, shatter, smash, split, rupture   heal

**frail**   weak, slight, delicate, fragile   strong

frame

**frame**   border, edge, trim

**frantic**   excited, hysterical, upset, frenzied   calm

**freak**   unusual, queer, grotesque, bizarre

**free**   1. release, clear, dismiss, discharge, liberate, acquit, emancipate   restrain

**free**   2. complimentary, gratis

**frequently**   often, regularly, repeatedly   seldom

**friend**   companion, buddy, pal   enemy

**frighten**   scare, alarm, terrify

**frosting**   icing, topping

**frosty**   icy, cold   hot

**frown**   pout, scowl   smile

**full**   packed, heaping, overflowing, loaded, stuffed, crowded, jammed, crammed   empty

**fun**   pleasure, entertainment, enjoyment

**funny**   amusing, entertaining, humorous, comical, laughable   sad

**fur**   pelt, hide, skin

**furious**   angry, annoyed, enraged, mad, infuriated   calm

**furnish**   supply, provide, equip, outfit

**fuse**   unite, join, combine, weld   separate

**fuss**   commotion, uproar, racket, riot, to-do, excitement

# G

**gadget**   contraption, tool, device, appliance

**gallant**   brave, bold, courageous, fearless, heroic   cowardly

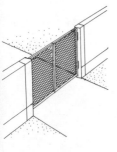

gate

gem

**gamble**   bet, wager, risk

**gang**   group, crew, ring, crowd, mob, band

**gap**   opening, hole, space

**garbage**   rubbish, trash, waste, junk, refuse

**garden**   plant, grow, raise, cultivate

**gash**   cut, wound, laceration

**gate**   fence, barrier

**gather**   collect, assemble, accumulate, amass, compile
scatter

**gay**   1. happy, lively, jolly, cheerful, jovial, vivacious
glum

**gay**   2. colorful, bright, vivid   dull

**gaze**   stare, gape, gawk

**gem**   jewel, precious stone, treasure

**general**   officer, commander

**generous**   giving, unselfish, kind, bighearted, liberal
selfish, stingy

**gentle**   soft, mild, tender, soothing   harsh, rough

**genuine**   real, true, pure, authentic   fake

**ghost**   spirit, phantom, spook

**giant**   colossal, huge, gigantic, vast, immense, enormous, mammoth   tiny

**gift**   1. present, offering

**gift**   2. talent, ability, forte

**gigantic**   colossal, huge, giant, vast, immense, enormous, mammoth   tiny

**giggle**   laugh, chuckle, snicker

**give**   present, hand over, provide, supply   take

**glacier**   iceberg

**glad**   happy, pleased, cheerful, delighted, joyful, satisfied   unhappy

**glamorous**   beautiful, attractive, stunning, gorgeous, dazzling   unattractive

**glance**   look, glimpse

**glare**   stare, scowl

**glaring**   bright, shining, glowing, flashing, dazzling, blinding   dim

**gleaming**   bright, shining, glowing, beaming, sparkling   dim

**glide**   move easily, slide, skim, coast

**globe**   sphere, earth, world, universe

**gloomy**   dark, dismal, dim, dreary, depressing, glum, bleak   cheerful

**glorious**   great, grand, magnificent, splendid, superb, majestic, wonderful, divine, sensational, marvelous

**glowing**   bright, shining, gleaming, beaming, sparkling   dim

**glue**   paste, cement, stick together

**glum**   sad, gloomy, depressed, moody   cheerful

**goal**   aim, object, target, purpose

glue

49

**gobble**   gulp, eat fast, devour

**good**   fine, nice, proper, right, appropriate, decent
bad

**gorgeous**   beautiful, stunning, glorious, dazzling,
ravishing   ugly

**govern**   rule, control, regulate, command, manage,
head, lead, supervise, direct, run

**grab**   snatch, seize, grasp, clutch

**gracious**   polite, pleasant, kindly, courteous, cordial,
friendly   rude, unkind

**grade**   1. mark, score

**grade**   2. class, division, group, category

**graduate**   pass, succeed, advance

**grand**   great, stately, majestic, magnificent, glorious,
splendid

**grant**   1. give, donate, contribute, present, award

**grant**   2. let, allow, permit   deny

**grasp**   grab, snatch, seize, clutch, grip, hold   release

**grateful**   thankful, appreciative   ungrateful

**grave**   burial place, plot

**grease**   oil, fat, lubrication

**great**   grand, magnificent, glorious, splendid, superb,
majestic, wonderful, sensational

**grimy**   dirty, filthy, soiled   clean

**grin**   smile, smirk

**grind**   crush, mash, crumble, squash, pulverize

**grip**   grasp, hold, seize, clutch

**gross**   crude, coarse, vulgar, unrefined   refined

**grotesque**   deformed, monstrous, disfigured, ugly, bizarre

**grouchy**   annoyed, cranky, cross, irritable, disagreeable, crabby, grumpy, moody   pleasant, cheerful

**group**   sort, classify, arrange, organize

**grow**   1. develop, mature, age, progress, increase   shrink

**grow**   2. plant, raise, cultivate

**growl**   snarl, grumble, complain

**guarantee**   promise, assure, pledge

**guard**   watch, protect, defend, shield, secure, patrol

guard

**guess**   think, believe, suppose, assume, imagine

**guest**   visitor, company

**guide**   1. show, direct, point out, lead, steer, escort

**guide**   2. manage, direct, control, regulate, advise, conduct

**guilty**   criminal, to blame, at fault   innocent

**gun**   weapon, firearm, pistol, revolver

gun

**gymnastics**   exercises, athletics, acrobatics, calisthenics

**gyp**   cheat, trick, deceive, swindle, defraud, dupe, bamboozle, mislead

**51**

# H

hammer (2)

**habit**　custom, practice, pattern, routine

**hall**　1. corridor, passageway, vestibule

**hall**　2. meeting room, auditorium

**halt**　stop, end, conclude, quit　start

**hammer**　1. pound, hit, knock, bang

**hammer**　2. mallet

**hand**　give, turn over, deliver, pass, transfer

**handbag**　purse, pocketbook

**handicap**　burden, disadvantage

**handle**　1. feel, touch, finger, manipulate

**handle**　2. manage, direct, carry on, run

**handsome**　good-looking, attractive　ugly

**handy**　1. useful, nearby, ready, available, convenient inconvenient

**handy**　2. skilled, expert, clever, apt, adept　clumsy, inept

**happen**　occur, take place

**happy**　glad, cheerful, contented, joyful, jolly, gay, pleased, satisfied　unhappy, sad

**harbor**   port, dock, pier, wharf

**hard**   1. firm, solid, stiff, rigid   soft

**hard**   2. difficult, tough, rough   easy

**hardly**   barely, scarcely, nearly

**hardy**   strong, tough, healthy, sturdy, rugged, robust
weak

**harm**   hurt, damage, injure, impair

**harsh**   cruel, severe, gruff, hard, rough, stern, tough,
curt, brusque   kind

**harvest**   crop, produce, output, yield

**hasty**   1. quick, fast, swift, rapid, speedy, hurried
slow

**hasty**   2. rash, reckless, impulsive

**hatch**   produce, breed, generate

**hate**   detest, despise, loathe   love

**haul**   drag, pull, tug, tow

**haunted**   spooky, weird, eerie, possessed

**hazardous**   dangerous, unsafe, risky   safe

**hazy**   1. dim, cloudy, misty, overcast, foggy   clear

**hazy**   2. unclear, vague, fuzzy, uncertain, confused
clear

**head**   lead, supervise, command, direct, manage, control, conduct, run

**heading**   title, headline

**heal**  cure, remedy, correct, mend, repair

**heaping**  full, overflowing, loaded, piled, stuffed, stacked

**heavy**  fat, stout, plump, hefty  thin

**hectic**  busy, exciting, frantic  calm

**help**  aid, assist, cooperate, support  hinder

**hem**  border, edge, rim

**heroic**  brave, bold, courageous, fearless, gallant  cowardly

**hide**  conceal, cover, mask, camouflage  reveal

**hideous**  ugly, horrible, dreadful, awful, ghastly, wretched  beautiful

high

**high**  tall, towering, elevated  low

**highway**  road, turnpike, expressway, thruway

**hilarious**  funny, humorous, laughable, comical

**hint**  clue, suggestion

**hire**  1. employ, engage  fire

**hire**  2. lease, rent, charter

**hit**  strike, bat, slap, smack, slug, swat

**hoist**  raise, lift, boost, elevate  lower

**hole**  gap, opening, cavity

**hollow**  empty, vacant

**home**  residence, dwelling

**homely**  ugly, plain, unattractive  attractive

**honest**   truthful, upright, moral, ethical, honorable, sincere   dishonest

**hook**   fasten, clip, latch, clasp, snap   unhook

**horrible**   dreadful, awful, terrible, frightful, ghastly, wretched

**hot**   1. steaming, sweltering, sizzling, torrid   cold

**hot**   2. spicy, sharp, peppery, tangy   bland

**house**   shelter, home, residence, dwelling

house

**howl**   cry, yell, shout, scream, screech, roar, wail

**hubbub**   noise, racket, commotion, disturbance, tumult, confusion, fuss, excitement, clamor, to-do   stillness, calm

**huddle**   crowd, gather, cluster, assemble

**hug**   embrace, grasp, hold, clutch, squeeze

**huge**   gigantic, colossal, giant, vast, immense, enormous, mammoth   tiny

**humble**   modest, plain, simple, unpretentious   showy

**humid**   moist, damp, muggy   dry

**humiliated**   embarrassed, ashamed, mortified

**humorous**   funny, laughable, comical, witty

**hunger**   appetite, craving, desire

**hunt**   seek, search, look, scout

**hurl**   toss, fling, throw, pitch

**hurry**   rush, hasten, speed, dash, hustle

55

hut

**hurt**   harm, damage, injure, impair

**husband**   spouse, mate, married man

**husky**   sturdy, rugged, muscular, strong, athletic   slight

**hut**   cabin, shed, shanty, shack

**hypnotize**   entrance, spellbind, mesmerize

**hysterical**   upset, uncontrollable, frantic, overexcited, delirious   calm

# I

icing

**icing**   frosting, topping

**idea**   thought, notion, concept

**identify**   name, describe, label, tag

**idiot**   imbecile, moron, half-wit, fool, simpleton

**ignore**   avoid, snub, overlook

**ill**   sick, ailing   healthy

**illegal**   unlawful, criminal   legal

**illustrate**   picture, draw, portray

**imagine**   1. think, guess, suppose, believe

**imagine**   2. dream, fantasize, envision

**imbecile**   idiot, moron, half-wit, fool, simpleton

**imitate**   copy, repeat, duplicate

**immediately**   now, instantly, at once, promptly   later

**immense**   huge, giant, enormous, vast, gigantic, colossal   tiny

**impatient**   restless, edgy   patient

**impolite**   rude, disrespectful, ill-mannered, insolent   polite

**important**   necessary, meaningful, significant, urgent, major   unimportant

**impossible**   unthinkable, absurd   possible

**improve**   better, perfect, advance

**incident**   event, happening, occurrence

**incinerator**   furnace, burner

**include**   contain, cover   exclude

**income**   earnings, wages, pay, salary

**incomplete**   unfinished, partial   complete

**inconsiderate**   thoughtless, unkind   considerate, thoughtful

**incorrect**   wrong, inaccurate, faulty, mistaken   right, correct

**increase**   enlarge, expand, extend, inflate   decrease

**incredible**   unbelievable, absurd, fantastic

**independent**   1. acting alone, self-reliant   dependent

**independent**   2. neutral, impartial

**indicate**   show, point out, demonstrate, express, signify

**indistinct**   unclear, vague, cloudy, dim, hazy, blurred
clear

**inexpensive**   cheap, low-priced, reasonable
expensive

**infect**   contaminate, pollute, poison

**inflate**   expand, stretch   deflate

**inflexible**   firm, rigid, stiff   flexible

**influence**   move, sway, persuade

**inform**   tell, notify, report, instruct

**information**   news, facts, knowledge, data

**infuriate**   anger, upset, enrage, irritate, provoke
soothe

**ingredient**   part, element, factor, component

**injure**   harm, hurt, damage, impair

**inn**   lodge, hotel, motel

**innocent**   blameless, without guilt   guilty

**inquire**   ask, question, investigate

**inquisitive**   curious, snooping, nosy

**insane**   crazy, mad, unbalanced   sane

**insignia**   emblems, symbols, badges

**insist**   urge, press, demand, push

**inspect**   examine, observe, study, review

inn

**inspire**   influence, encourage

**instantly**   immediately, fast, promptly, quickly, rapidly, swiftly

**institution**   organization, establishment

**instruct**   teach, show, educate, inform, tell, advise

**instrument**   tool, device, implement, utensil, gadget, appliance

**insult**   offend, affront

**intelligent**   bright, smart, alert, wise   ignorant

**interesting**   entertaining, amusing, fascinating, absorbing, captivating   boring, uninteresting

**interfere**   intrude, meddle

**intermission**   recess, pause, break, interval

**interpret**   explain, clarify

**interrupt**   break in, interfere, intrude

**interview**   question, quiz, interrogate

**intrude**   interfere, meddle

**invade**   raid, attack, overrun

**invalid**   sickly, weak, unhealthy, frail   healthy

**invent**   make up, develop, originate, create, produce, discover, devise

**investigate**   look into, explore, examine, inspect, study, probe

**invite**   ask, call

**irritable**   cross, cranky, annoyed, grouchy, disagreeable   pleasant

**irritate** 1. annoy, bother, anger, infuriate, provoke
**irritate** 2. rub, chafe, inflame   soothe
**issue** 1. topic, subject, theme, question, point
**issue** 2. copy, edition

# J

**jab** poke, push, thrust
**jail** lock up, imprison, incarcerate
**jam** 1. crowd, stuff, cram, squeeze, crush, load
**jam** 2. jelly, marmalade, preserve
**jealous** envious
**jewel** gem, stone
**job** work, employment, task, assignment, duty, occupation, position
**jog** run, sprint
**join** connect, unite, combine, link, attach   separate, detach
**jolly** merry, cheerful, jovial, gay, happy, pleasant   glum
**journey** expedition, trip, excursion, pilgrimage

jog

**joyful**   jolly, merry, cheerful, jovial, gay, happy   glum

**judge**   referee, umpire, mediator

**jumble**   mix, scramble

**jumbo**   gigantic, colossal, huge, giant, immense, enormous   tiny

**jump**   spring, leap, bound

**junk**   rubbish, trash, scrap

**just**   fair, proper, moral   unjust

**juvenile**   young, youthful   old

jump

# K

**keep**   save, preserve, conserve   discard

**kennel**   doghouse, pound

**key**   1. clue, hint, evidence, lead, explanation

**key**   2. pitch, tone, note

**kid**   1. tease, fool, joke, jest

**kid**   2. child, tot

**kidnap**   snatch, abduct

**kill**   slay, murder, slaughter, execute, assassinate

**kind**   1. considerate, thoughtful, sympathetic, gentle, helpful   unkind, mean

kid (2)

**61**

knife

**kind**  2. sort, type, variety

**king**  ruler, chief, monarch, sovereign

**kit**  equipment, set, furnishings, gear

**knife**  blade, sword

**knock**  hit, strike, beat, hammer, rap, bang

# L

**label**  tag, name, title

**labor**  work, toil

**lack**  want, need, require

**ladle**  dipper, scoop

**land**  arrive, touch down, descend

**lane**  path, road, aisle

**large**  big, huge, tremendous, enormous, immense, grand, massive  small

**lariat**  rope, lasso

**lasso**  rope, lariat

**last**  final, end  first, beginning

**latch**  lock, hook, clasp, fastener

lariat

**laugh**  giggle, chuckle

**launch**  start, begin, introduce, establish

**law**  rule, regulation, principle, act, ordinance

**lay**  put, place, set

**lazy**  lax, idle, inactive  active

**lead**  guide, conduct, manage, direct, head

**league**  union, group, alliance

**leap**  jump, spring, bound

**learn**  1. find out, discover

**learn**  2. memorize

**lease**  rent, hire, charter

**leash**  strap, chain

**least**  fewest, smallest, minimum  most

**leave**  1. go, depart, exit  arrive

**leave**  2. quit, abandon, desert  stay

**lecture**  speech, talk, address

**ledge**  shelf, edge

ledge

**legal**  lawful, permitted, allowed, legitimate, authorized  illegal

**legend**  story, tale, fable, myth

**lend**  give, loan  borrow

**lengthen**  extend, stretch, prolong  shorten

**less**  fewer, smaller  more

**lesson**  assignment, exercise

Dear Mom and Dad,
Camp is great.
There are seven kids
in my bunk.
Our counselor is nice.
I learned to paddle
a canoe.   Love,
         Anna

letter

**let**   permit, allow, consent

**letter**   message, note, dispatch

**level**   flat, even, smooth   uneven

**liberty**   freedom, independence, emancipation

**license**   permission, consent, approval, authorization

**lid**   cover, top, cap

**lie**   fib, exaggerate

**lift**   hoist, raise, boost, elevate   lower

**light**   1. bright, clear   dark

**light**   2. weightless, airy, delicate   heavy

**like**   enjoy, admire, appreciate   dislike

**limit**   end, boundary, restriction

**link**   join, connect, unite, combine, attach, bridge
   separate

**liquid**   fluid   solid

**list**   record, enumerate

**litter**   rubbish, scrap, junk, trash, garbage

**little**   small, tiny, minute, slight   big

**live**   dwell, reside

**lively**   active, energetic, animated, vivacious, spry,
   spirited, gay   dull

**load**   1. burden, cargo, freight

**load**   2. fill, stuff, pack   unload

**loaf**   idle, lounge, loiter

**loan**   give, lend

**lobby**   entrance, vestibule

**location**   area, place, site, spot, region

**lock**   fasten, close, hook, clasp, latch, shut   unlock, open

lock

**logical**   reasonable, sensible, rational   unreasonable

**lonely**   alone, friendless, isolated

**look**   1. see, glance, gaze, stare

**look**   2. seem, appear

**loose**   slack, limp, drooping   tight

**lose**   1. fail, flop, be unsuccessful   win

**lose**   2. misplace, mislay   find

**lottery**   raffle, drawing

**loud**   noisy, thunderous, roaring   soft

**love**   adore, idolize, cherish, admire   hate

**lovely**   attractive, pleasing, pretty, delightful, charming, appealing, beautiful   unattractive

**loyal**   faithful, true, devoted, trustworthy   disloyal

**lucky**   fortunate   unlucky

**luggage**   baggage, bags, suitcases, valises

luggage

**luxurious**   extravagant, elegant, magnificent, grand, splendid

# M

**mad**  1. crazy, insane, deranged  sane

**mad**  2. angry, furious, enraged, annoyed, cross, irritated

**magazine**  periodical, journal

**magic**  witchcraft, voodoo, wizardry, sorcery

**magnetic**  attractive, pulling, drawing

**magnificent**  grand, great, stately, majestic, glorious, splendid, superb, exquisite, marvelous, wonderful

**magnify**  enlarge, expand, exaggerate, stretch, inflate, increase, amplify  minimize

**maid**  servant, housekeeper, domestic

**mail**  1. send, dispatch

**mail**  2. letters, correspondence

**main**  chief, principal, foremost, leading

**make**  1. build, construct, create, manufacture, produce, form, assemble

**make**  2. force, cause, compel

**make**  3. kind, type, sort, brand

maid

mail (2)

**manage**  conduct, direct, lead, guide, run, operate, control, govern, supervise

**manner**  way, style, nature, character, method

**manual**  guidebook, handbook, directory

**manufacture**  make, build, construct, create, produce, form, assemble

**many**  numerous, various, several  few

**map**  chart

map

**marathon**  race, contest

**march**  walk, hike, parade

**margin**  border, edge, rim

**marionette**  puppet, doll

**mark**  grade, rating

**market**  store, shop, mart

**marvelous**  wonderful, extraordinary, glorious, great, grand, magnificent, splendid, superb, divine, sensational, spectacular  ordinary

**mash**  crush, crumble, grind, pulverize

**mask**  disguise, camouflage

marionette

**masquerade**  disguise, pretend, pose, impersonate

**master**  head, chief, ruler, commander

**match**  contest, game, battle

**mature**  full-grown, adult, developed, ripe  immature

**maximum**  most, greatest, largest  minimum

**maybe**  perhaps, possibly

**67**

meadow

**meadow**  pasture, field, grassland

**mean**  1. suggest, signify, imply

**mean**  2. unkind, cross, irritable, malicious  kind

**mechanic**  repairman, technician

**medal**  award, prize, honor, medallion

**medicine**  drug, cure, remedy

**meek**  shy, timid, gentle, tame, mild, modest  aggressive

**meet**  assemble, gather, congregate, unite

**melody**  tune, song

**melt**  soften, dissolve

**mend**  fix, repair, adjust, regulate  break

**merchandise**  goods, products, wares

**merchant**  storekeeper, dealer

**merge**  combine, unite, mix, blend, join, fuse  separate

**merry**  gay, happy, lively, jolly, cheerful, jovial  glum

**message**  word, report, communication, dispatch

**messy**  sloppy, careless, untidy, dirty  neat

**meter**  gauge, measure

**method**  plan, manner, means, system, way, style, procedure

**microscopic**  tiny, minute  huge

**middle**  center, heart, core, hub

**mighty**  strong, powerful, great, grand  weak

**mild**  gentle, calm, moderate  harsh

**military**   army, troops, soldiers, armed forces

**mimic**   copy, imitate, mock, mime, ape

**mind**   1. brain, intellect

**mind**   2. watch, tend, look after

**miniature**   small, tiny, minute   giant

**minimum**   least, smallest   maximum

**minister**   clergyman, pastor, chaplain

**1. minute**   instant, moment

**2. minute**   tiny, small, miniature   giant

**miraculous**   remarkable, wonderful, marvelous, extraordinary, incredible

**mischievous**   naughty, devilish, playful

**miserable**   1. sad, unhappy, downcast   happy

**miserable**   2. wretched, mean   pleasant

**misfortune**   trouble, difficulty, mishap, sorrow

**mislead**   deceive, trick, dupe

**misplace**   lose, mislay

**missile**   rocket, projectile

missile

**missing**   lost, absent, gone   present

**mission**   job, errand, task, assignment, chore, duty

**mistake**   error, fault, slip, blunder, oversight

**mistreat**   abuse, molest, manhandle

**misty**   cloudy, foggy, smoky   clear

**misunderstanding** difficulty, difference, disagreement

**mix** blend, combine, join, stir, scramble   separate

**moan** groan, complain, wail

**mob** crowd, throng, horde

**model** duplicate, reproduction, likeness, replica

**modern** new, up-to-date, advanced, contemporary, recent   old-fashioned

**modest** humble, bashful, shy, quiet   bold

**moist** damp, wet, soggy   dry

**mold** 1. shape, form, carve, sculpture

**mold** 2. decay, rot, spoil

**molest** harm, mistreat, annoy, abuse

**moment** instant, minute

**monarch** ruler, king, sovereign

**money** currency, cash

money

**monitor** helper, assistant

**monotonous** boring, dull, tedious, humdrum   interesting

**monster** fiend, ogre, demon, freak

**mood** feeling, temperament, disposition

**moody** gloomy, glum, depressed, temperamental, sullen

**mop** scrub, swab

**motion**   movement, activity
**mountain**   hill, elevation
**movement**   motion, activity
**mow**   cut, clip, crop, shear
**mud**   slime, dirt, muck
**muggy**   humid, damp, sticky, dank
**murder**   kill, slay, slaughter, execute, assassinate
**mutiny**   rebellion, revolt, riot, uprising
**mystery**   puzzle, problem
**myth**   fable, story, fairy tale, legend

mow

# N

**nag**   pester, annoy, bother
**nail**   fasten, attach, fix, secure
**naked**   uncovered, undressed, nude, bare   covered
**name**   label, tag, title
**nap**   sleep, doze, drowse, snooze
**narcotics**   drugs, opiates
**narrator**   storyteller
**narrow**   cramped, confined, limited, restricted, close, tight   wide

nap

**nasty**   unpleasant, disgusting, repulsive, offensive, obnoxious   pleasant, delightful

**nation**   country, land

**natural**   genuine, real, pure   artificial

**naturally**   certainly, surely, of course

**naughty**   bad, disobedient, mischievous   good, obedient

**near**   close, at hand   far

**nearly**   almost, close to

**neat**   tidy, orderly, well-kept   sloppy, messy

**necessary**   needed, important, essential, urgent, required   unnecessary

**need**   want, lack, require

**neglected**   overlooked, ignored, slighted   protected

**neighborhood**   area, surroundings, vicinity, environment

**nerve**   courage, daring

**nervous**   restless, upset, disturbed, shaken, flustered, tense, edgy, jittery   calm

**new**   modern, current, up-to-date, recent   old

**nice**   pleasant, agreeable, good, fine   unpleasant

**noise**   racket, clamor, commotion, uproar   quiet

**nominate**   name, select, choose, designate

**nonsense**   foolishness, stupidity, rubbish, bunk

**normal**  regular, usual, typical, standard, ordinary
unusual, abnormal

**nosy**  snoopy, curious, prying

**note**  memo, message

**notice**  see, observe, note

**notify**  tell, report, advise, inform

**now**  immediately, instantly, at once, promptly, presently  later

**nudge**  encourage, urge, prod, push, prompt, inspire

**nuisance**  pest, annoyance

**numb**  unfeeling, deadened

**number**  1. quantity, count, amount

**number**  2. numeral, figure, symbol, digit

**numeral**  number, figure, symbol, digit

**numerous**  many, a lot, several, various  few

**nurse**  care for, tend to, nurture

**nutrition**  food, nourishment

note

# O

**oath**  pledge, promise, vow

**obey**  listen to, mind, comply  disobey

**1. object**  1. thing, article, item

**object**  2. goal, purpose, aim, target

**2. object**  complain, protest, disagree, challenge, disapprove  approve, agree

**obnoxious**  nasty, unpleasant, disgusting, hateful, disagreeable, repulsive, offensive  pleasant, agreeable

**observe**  see, look, watch, study, examine

**obstacle**  barrier, block, snag, obstruction

**obstinate**  stubborn, willful, headstrong, pigheaded, ornery  flexible

**obstruction**  obstacle, barrier, block, snag

**obtain**  get, receive, gain, acquire

**obvious**  plain, clear, evident, apparent  vague, unclear

**occupation**  business, work, job, profession, employment, trade

**occur**  happen, take place, transpire

**odd**  strange, unusual, peculiar, queer, weird, bizarre  ordinary

**odor**  smell, scent, aroma, fragrance

**office**  1. workplace, studio, headquarters

**office**  2. position, post, role

**often**  many times, frequently, repeatedly  seldom

**ogre**   monster, fiend, demon

**old**   aged, elderly   young

**omit**   leave out, miss, skip, exclude   include

**only**   just, simply, merely

**ooze**   seep, leak

**open**   start, begin, launch, establish   close

**operate**   work, run, manage, handle

**opinion**   belief, judgment, feeling, sentiment, attitude, view, thought

old

**opponent**   enemy, competitor, rival, adversary   ally

**opportunity**   chance, occasion

**oppose**   fight, disagree, argue, dispute, quarrel, contradict, resist   agree

**optimistic**   hopeful, cheerful, bright, lighthearted, carefree   pessimistic

**oral**   spoken, voiced, verbal

**orbit**   path, circuit, circle, revolution

**order**   1. arrangement, manner, system

**order**   2. command, instruction, directive

**ordinary**   usual, common, normal, average, everyday   unusual

**organize**   set up, arrange, classify, systematize, categorize

ornament

**original**  1. firsthand, authentic   copied

**original**  2. novel, new, fresh, different, unique
  ordinary

**ornament**  decoration, trimming, adornment

**ornery**  1. stubborn, obstinate, willful, headstrong,
  pigheaded   flexible

**ornery**  2. mean, cranky, grouchy, cross, difficult
  pleasant, agreeable

**outcome**  result, effect, end, conclusion, consequence

**outfit**  equip, provide, furnish, supply

**outing**  trip, journey, tour, jaunt, excursion

**outline**  plan, sketch, diagram, draft

**outlook**  view, attitude, position

**outrageous**  absurd, unbelievable, ridiculous, shocking,
  extreme, ludicrous   ordinary, sensible

**outstanding**  important, well-known, great, distinguished, famous, celebrated, prominent   ordinary,
  unimportant

**overcast**  cloudy, dark, dismal   clear

**overcome**  conquer, defeat, upset, overpower, sur-
  mount   surrender, yield

**overlook**  ignore, neglect, disregard, skip, miss

**overpass**  bridge, span, viaduct

**oversight**  error, slip, omission

76

**overthrow**   defeat, overcome, overpower, destroy, upset

**own**   have, possess

# P

**pace**   rate, speed

**pack**   fill, load, stuff   empty

**pact**   agreement, understanding, treaty

**pad**   1. notebook, tablet

**pad**   2. pillow, cushion

**pageant**   show, exhibition, parade, display, review, spectacle

pad (1)

**pail**   bucket

**pain**   ache, hurt, discomfort, soreness, pang

**paint**   1. coat, color, cover

**paint**   2. picture, draw, illustrate, portray, depict

**pair**   set, couple, two

**pal**   friend, companion, buddy, chum

**palace**   castle, mansion, château

**pale**   faint, colorless, wan, pallid   bright

**pamphlet**   booklet, brochure, leaflet, folder

palace

**77**

**panic**   fear, fright, dread, alarm, terror

**pants**   trousers, slacks

**parade**   procession, march, display, review, pageant

**parched**   dry, thirsty, arid, dehydrated

**pardon**   forgive, excuse, absolve   blame

**part**   1. portion, section, segment, piece

**part**   2. role, character

**participate**   take part in, partake, contribute, join

**particular**   fussy, critical, exacting

**partner**   companion, associate, colleague, collaborator

**party**   celebration, festivity

party

**pass**   1. do well, succeed   fail

**pass**   2. deliver, hand over, transfer

**pass**   3. throw, toss, fling, hurl, pitch

**passage**   corridor, lane, opening, channel

**paste**   glue, mucilage, adhesive

**patch**   mend, repair, fix

**path**   route, way, track, trail, lane, road

**patience**   tolerance, understanding, self-control
impatience

**patriotic**   loyal, nationalistic

**patrol**   watch, guard, protect, police

**pattern**   1. design, picture, print

**pattern**   2. model, example

path

**78**

**pause** wait, stop, rest, recess  continue

**peaceful** quiet, calm, still, serene  hectic

**peak** top, crest, tip, summit  base

**peculiar** odd, strange, unusual, queer  ordinary, normal

**peddle** sell, vend, hawk

**pedestrian** walker

**peek** glance, look, glimpse

**penalty** punishment, fine

**penmanship** handwriting, script

**pennant** flag, banner, streamer

**pep** energy, spirit, vim, vigor

**perfect** faultless, flawless, ideal, excellent  imperfect, defective

**perform** do, carry out, achieve, accomplish

**perhaps** maybe, possibly, conceivably

**period** time, span, interval

**perish** die, expire, succumb

**permanent** steady, lasting, unchanging, constant  temporary

**permit** allow, let, consent

**personal** private, individual

**perspire** sweat

**persuade** win over, convince

peddle

pennant

79

pet (2)

**pessimistic**   unhappy, hopeless, gloomy, downhearted   optimistic

**pester**   annoy, bother, disturb, tease, nag, harass

**pet**   1. favorite, choice

**pet**   2. stroke, pat, caress, fondle

**petite**   little, small, slight, tiny   big

**petrified**   1. scared, frightened, terrified, horrified, shocked, stunned

**petrified**   2. hardened, stonelike, solidified

**petty**   unimportant, small, minor, trivial   important

**phantom**   ghost, spirit, vision, spook, fantasy, illusion

**pharmacist**   druggist, chemist

**photograph**   snapshot, picture

**physician**   doctor, medic

**pick**   choose, select, elect, opt

**picture**   illustration, drawing, representation

**piece**   part, portion, section, segment, bit, chunk, hunk

**pier**   dock, wharf

**pierce**   stab, puncture, penetrate

**pile**   heap, stack, mound, load, collection

**pillow**   cushion, headrest

**pin**   fasten, attach, clasp, clip

**pioneer**   settler, colonist

**pistol**   gun, revolver, firearm

picture

80

**pitch**   toss, fling, throw, hurl, cast

**pity**   sympathy, compassion

**place**   put, lay, set, deposit, arrange

**plain**   1. clear, simple, understandable, distinct
complicated

**plain**   2. unattractive, homely   pretty

**plan**   intend, aim, propose

**playful**   frisky, lively, gay, spirited, impish   serious

**pleasant**   pleasing, likable, appealing, agreeable,
cheerful, delightful, charming, satisfying
unpleasant

**pledge**   promise, vow, oath, agreement

**plenty**   a lot, sufficient, enough, ample   insufficient

**plot**   plan, scheme, concoct

**plug**   block, clog, stop, jam, obstruct   open, clear

**plump**   chubby, fat, stout, stocky, heavy, pudgy,
chunky   thin

**plunge**   dive, fall, plummet

**poetry**   rhyme, verse

**point**   direct, show, indicate

**poisonous**   toxic, deadly, venomous

**poke**   jab, push, shove, thrust

**police**   guard, watch, protect, defend, shield, secure,
patrol

polish

pound

**polish** shine, buff, rub, wax, glaze

**polite** well-mannered, courteous, respectful, gracious rude

**poll** survey, vote, questionnaire

**polluted** contaminated, impure, foul, dirty, poisoned clean, pure

**poor** penniless, needy, impoverished, destitute rich

**popular** 1. common unusual

**popular** 2. well-liked, favorite, admired unpopular, disliked

**portable** movable, mobile, transferable stationary

**portion** part, section, segment, piece, share

**position** 1. place, spot, location

**position** 2. job, role, function

**positive** sure, certain, definite unsure

**possessions** belongings, property

**possible** likely, probable, feasible impossible

**post** 1. list, notify, announce

**post** 2. job, position, duty, assignment

**postpone** put off, delay, stall, procrastinate

**pound** beat, strike, hit, punch, knock, rap, bang, pummel

**power** 1. strength, might, force, vigor, energy

**power** 2. authority, control, influence

**practically**  almost, nearly, approximately

**practice**  drill, exercise, train, rehearse

**praise**  compliment, commend, flatter

**precious**  1. valuable, expensive, costly, priceless
cheap

**precious**  2. special, loved, adored, cherished

**precipitation**  rain, snow, moisture

**precise**  exact, accurate, definite  approximate

**predicament**  mess, dilemma, plight

**predict**  forecast, foresee, prophesy

**prefer**  favor, like, fancy

**prejudiced**  partial, biased  fair, neutral

**prepare**  get ready, fix, arrange, concoct

**present**  gift, offering

present

**preserve**  keep, save, hold, maintain, conserve, protect,
guard  destroy, neglect

**press**  1. push, force, squeeze, clasp

**press**  2. iron, smooth

**pretend**  make believe, act, fake, bluff, feign

**pretty**  attractive, lovely, good-looking  homely,
unattractive

**prevent**  stop, block, keep from, deter  allow

**price**  cost, value, amount

**pride**  self-respect, self-esteem, dignity

**primitive**  1. original, ancient, prehistoric   modern
**primitive**  2. uncivilized, crude, barbaric
**principal**  chief, main, leading
**principle**  rule, law, belief
**print**  publish, issue
**prison**  jail, penitentiary, reformatory
**private**  personal, secret, hidden, intimate   public
**privilege**  advantage, right
**prize**  award, reward, treasure
**problem**  question, issue
**procedure**  plan, practice, rule, policy, way, custom
**proceed**  go ahead, progress, advance
**produce**  make, create, manufacture
**profession**  job, work, occupation, career, vocation
**program**  schedule, plan, list, agenda
**progress**  go ahead, proceed, advance
**prohibit**  forbid, bar, ban, prevent   allow
**project**  undertaking, enterprise, venture
**promise**  agree, swear, pledge, guarantee, vow
**promising**  hopeful, encouraging, favorable
**prompt**  1. punctual, on time   late
**prompt**  2. remind, coach, cue
**proper**  correct, right, appropriate, fitting, decent, suitable   wrong, improper

**property**   possessions, holdings, belongings

**prosperous**   successful, comfortable, well-off, rich, wealthy, affluent   poor

**protect**   defend, safeguard, shield, support, cover

**protest**   object, complain, challenge

**proud**   pleased, gratified

**prove**   show, demonstrate, document

**provide**   supply, give, furnish

**provoke**   annoy, bother, disturb, tease, taunt, irritate, anger, antagonize

**pry**   1. meddle, mix, snoop

**pry**   2. loosen, jimmy

**publish**   print, issue

**pull**   tug, tow, draw, drag, yank, haul   push

**punch**   beat, strike, hit, pound, knock, batter, wallop, slug, pummel

**punctual**   prompt, on time   late

**puncture**   pierce, stab, penetrate

**punish**   discipline, correct, chastise

**pupil**   student

**purchase**   buy, acquire   sell

**purify**   cleanse, clarify, refine, filter   soil, pollute

**purpose**   goal, aim, object, target

**push**   press, thrust, shove, force, nudge   pull

protest

pull

pupil

85

**put**   place, lay, set, deposit
**puzzle**   mystery, problem, enigma

# Q

quarrel

**quaint**   charming, old-fashioned
**quake**   shake, tremble, vibrate, shudder
**qualified**   able, capable, fit, competent, suited   unfit
**quality**   trait, feature, characteristic
**quantity**   amount, sum, number
**quarrel**   argue, fight, disagree, differ, dispute, bicker
   agree
**queer**   odd, strange, peculiar, unusual, weird   normal
**question**   ask, inquire, interrogate   answer
**quick**   1. fast, rapid, swift, speedy   slow
**quick**   2. bright, alert, smart, sharp, keen   dull, slow
**quiet**   silent, still, hushed   noisy
**quit**   stop, end, cease, halt, conclude, discontinue,
   finish   continue
**quiver**   shake, tremble, shiver
**quiz**   test, examination
**quote**   repeat, echo, cite

86

# R

**race**   1. run, speed, rush, dash, hurry, sprint

**race**   2. nationality, ancestry

**racket**   1. noise, commotion, uproar, hubbub, din, clamor, disturbance   quiet

**racket**   2. fraud, swindle

**rage**   1. anger, violence, frenzy, furor, fit

**rage**   2. fad, style, fashion

**ragged**   torn, worn, shabby, tattered, frayed, seedy

**raid**   attack, invade, assault

**raise**   1. lift, elevate, boost, hoist   lower

**raise**   2. produce, rear

**rake**   collect, gather

**rank**   grade, class, position

**rapid**   fast, swift, speedy, quick, hasty   slow

**rare**   scarce, uncommon, unusual, unique   common

**rate**   grade, evaluate, rank, appraise

**raw**   uncooked   cooked

race (1)

**ray**   light, beam, gleam

**react**   respond, answer

**ready**   prepared, set   unprepared

**real**   genuine, true, authentic, actual   fake

**realize**   understand, grasp, comprehend

**rear**   1. back, hind   front

**rear**   2. raise, produce

**reason**   explanation, cause, motive, basis, justification

**reasonable**   fair, sensible, just, sound, practical, realistic, rational   unreasonable, unfair

**rebel**   disobey, defy, riot, revolt   obey

**recall**   remember, recollect, review, reminisce   forget

**receive**   take in, get, gain, obtain   give

**recent**   new, modern, current, up-to-date, late   old

**recess**   pause, stop, rest

**recipe**   instructions, directions, formula

**recite**   tell, relate, narrate, repeat

**reckless**   careless, sloppy, thoughtless, rash, hasty, wild, inconsiderate   careful

**recognize**   know, acknowledge

**recommend**   suggest, advise, advocate

**record**   write, list, enter, log

**recover**   1. get back, regain, rescue, reclaim, retrieve   lose

**recover**   2. get better, improve, heal, rally, recuperate

record

88

**recreation**  play, amusement, entertainment, pleasure, enjoyment, fun

**reduce**  decrease, lessen, cut  increase

**referee**  judge, umpire, mediator

**reform**  improve, change, revise

**refrigerate**  cool, chill

**refund**  repay, reimburse

**regal**  royal, majestic, stately, noble, grand

**region**  district, area, section, location, territory, vicinity, zone

referee

**register**  sign up, enlist, enroll, join

**regular**  common, ordinary, usual, familiar, everyday, typical, normal  unusual

**rehearse**  drill, train, practice, repeat, prepare

**reject**  discard, refuse, exclude, eliminate, bar  accept

**relate**  tell, recite, narrate, repeat, report, state, recount

**related**  connected, associated, akin

**relax**  rest, unwind

**release**  let go, dismiss, discharge, free  hold

**reliable**  dependable, trustworthy  unreliable

**relief**  1. help, assistance, aid

**relief**  2. ease, alleviation

**relief**  3. change, substitution, replacement, alternate

relax

**religious**  pious, devout

**rely**  depend, count

**remain**  stay, continue

**remark**  statement, comment

**remarkable**  extraordinary, great, special, unusual, exceptional, noteworthy, memorable  ordinary

**remedy**  cure, treatment, relief

**remember**  recall, recollect, review, reminisce  forget

**remove**  take away, eliminate, discard, withdraw  leave

**rent**  lease, let, hire

**repair**  mend, fix, adjust, patch, restore, service  break

**repeat**  duplicate, echo

**reply**  answer, response

**report**  tell, recite, narrate, state, describe, recount

**request**  ask for, apply for

**require**  need, lack, want

**rescue**  save, recover, free, salvage

**research**  exploration, investigation, inquiry, probe

**resemblance**  likeness, similarity

**reserve**  keep, save, hold, put aside

**resign**  give up, leave, quit

**respect**  admire, appreciate, value, honor

rescue

**respond**   reply, answer, react

**responsible**   reliable, dependable, trustworthy
  irresponsible

**rest**   1. pause, relax, unwind

**rest**   2. remains, balance, leftovers

**restless**   impatient, edgy, uneasy, fidgety   calm,
  composed

**restore**   renew, renovate, repair

**restriction**   limitation, restraint

**result**   outcome, end, effect, consequence

**retire**   resign, leave, quit

**return**   1. go back, revisit

**return**   2. give back, repay

**reunion**   get-together, gathering, meeting

**reveal**   show, expose, display, disclose   hide

**review**   study, remember, recall, learn

**revive**   bring back, resuscitate

**revolution**   1. revolt, riot, rebellion, uprising

**revolution**   2. circle, orbit

**reward**   award, payment, prize, compensation

**rhythm**   beat, tempo

**rich**   wealthy, comfortable, well-to-do, affluent, prosperous   poor

rip

road

**ridiculous** foolish, silly, stupid, outrageous, absurd, unbelievable sensible

**right** correct, accurate, good, fitting, suitable, proper, valid, sound wrong

**rigid** stiff, firm, unbending, hard soft, flexible

**rim** edge, border, frame, fringe

**riot** rebellion, revolt, uprising, brawl

**rip** tear, cut, split, slit, slash

**ripe** ready, developed, mature, full-grown green, undeveloped

**risk** chance, gamble

**road** path, route, way, thoroughfare

**roam** wander, drift, meander, ramble, rove

**rob** steal, loot, burglarize

**role** part, character

**room** space, leeway

**rot** spoil, decay

**rotate** spin, turn, gyrate, swivel, pivot

**rough** 1. bumpy, coarse, uneven, jagged, choppy smooth

**rough** 2. crude, harsh, rowdy, tough gentle

**route** course, path, rounds

**routine** habit, system, custom, practice, pattern

92

**rove**   roam, wander, drift, meander, ramble

**row**   1. line, series, column, string

**row**   2. paddle

**rowdy**   rough, disorderly, disobedient, boisterous  well-behaved

**royal**   regal, majestic, stately, noble, grand

**rubbish**   waste, garbage, trash, refuse, scrap, junk

rubbish

**rude**   impolite, disrespectful, discourteous, crude,  ill-mannered, curt, insolent   polite

**rug**   carpet, mat

**ruin**   spoil, destroy, wreck, demolish, ravage

**rule**   1. govern, control, regulate, command, manage,  head, lead, supervise, direct, run, guide

**rule**   2. regulation, law

**rumor**   gossip, talk

**run**   1. race, hurry, hasten, jog, sprint

**run**   2. govern, control, regulate, command, manage,  head, lead, supervise, direct

**run**   3. operate, work

**run**   4. flow, stream, pour, gush

**run**   5. campaign, electioneer

**rush**   hurry, hasten, speed, dash, hustle

**rusty**   corroded

**ruthless**   cruel, mean, heartless, brutal, savage   kind

# S

**sacred**   religious, holy, spiritual

**sad**   unhappy, depressed, downhearted, blue, sorrow-ful, downcast, gloomy, glum, forlorn, dejected, melan-choly   happy

**safe**   secure, protected, guarded   dangerous

**sag**   droop, hang, drag

**salary**   pay, wages, compensation

**sample**   test, try, experiment

**sand**   scrape, smooth, file, grind

**sane**   sound, rational, sensible, logical

**sanitary**   clean, hygienic, sterile   dirty, unsanitary

**sarcastic**   cutting, bitter, sharp, stinging

**satisfied**   pleased, content, gratified   displeased

**save**   1. keep, preserve, conserve, store, accumulate   spend, discard

**save**   2. rescue, recover, retrieve

**say**   speak, tell, declare, state, exclaim, express, re-mark, comment, mention, utter

**scald**  burn, scorch

**scar**  blemish, mark, wound

**scarce**  rare, scanty, sparse  plentiful

**scare**  frighten, alarm, startle, shock, unnerve, terrify
calm, soothe

**scatter**  spread, disperse, distribute  gather

**scene**  view, sight, setting, picture, vista

**scent**  odor, smell, aroma, fragrance

**schedule**  program, plan, list, agenda, slate, line-up

**scheme**  plot, plan, conspiracy

**scold**  reprimand, chide, admonish

scold

**scorch**  burn, singe, sear, char

**score**  count, sum, tally, total

**scoundrel**  rascal, devil, imp, scamp, villain

**scout**  hunt, seek, search

**scramble**  mix, blend, combine, jumble  separate

**scrap**  1. small amount, shred, speck, fragment

**scrap**  2. litter, rubbish, junk, trash, garbage, waste,
debris

**scrape**  rub

scrape

**scratch**  cut, mark, scrape, scar

**scream**  yell, howl, cry, shout, screech, wail, shriek

**screech**  shriek, scream, yell, howl, cry, shout, wail,
squeal

seal (3)

**screen**  guard, shield, net
**scribble**  scrawl, scratch
**script**  writing, penmanship
**scrub**  scour, clean, rub, wash
**sculpture**  carve, mold, shape, form, chisel
**seal**  1. fasten, secure, bind, close, shut  open
**seal**  2. stamp, sign, mark
**seal**  3. sea lion
**sear**  scorch, burn, singe, char
**search**  scout, hunt, seek
**season**  flavor, spice
**secret**  private, hidden, secluded
**section**  part, portion, segment, piece
**secure**  safe, protected, guarded  unsafe, insecure
**seek**  search, scout, hunt
**seem**  appear, look
**seep**  ooze, leak, trickle
**segment**  section, part, portion, piece, division
**seize**  grab, grasp, snatch, clutch  release
**seldom**  rarely, hardly, infrequently  often
**select**  choose, pick, opt
**self-conscious**  shy, timid, bashful, embarrassed
  confident
**selfish**  self-centered, greedy, possessive  generous,
  good-natured

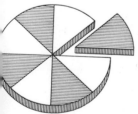

segment

96

**sell** peddle, vend  buy

**send** dispatch, forward, transmit  receive

**sensational** marvelous, wonderful, extraordinary, glorious, great, grand, magnificent, splendid, superb, divine, spectacular, exciting, thrilling  ordinary, dull

**senseless** foolish, silly, dumb, stupid, inane  sensible

**sensible** reasonable, logical, practical, realistic, wise, intelligent  foolish

**separate** divide, split, part, sort, isolate  join, unite

**sequel** follow-up, continuation

**serious** 1. solemn, grave, somber, grim  gay, carefree

**serious** 2. important, major, significant, meaningful  unimportant

**sermon** lecture, talk

**serpent** snake, viper

serpent

**set** 1. place, put, lay, deposit, arrange

**set** 2. fix, adjust, regulate

**settle** 1. decide, resolve, reconcile

**settle** 2. locate, occupy, live

**several** many, numerous, various, some  few

**severe** harsh, cruel, hard, rough, tough, extreme  mild

**shabby** ragged, torn, worn, shoddy, tattered, frayed, seedy

**97**

shack

shampoo

shore

**shack**  hut, cabin, shanty

**shake**  tremble, shudder, shiver, quiver, vibrate

**shameful**  awful, disgraceful, humiliating, scandalous

**shampoo**  soap, lather, wash

**shape**  form, make, develop, fashion, create, construct, mold, design

**share**  divide, split, distribute, apportion

**sharp**  1. pointy, angular   dull

**sharp**  2. bright, clever, smart, alert, quick-witted, keen, shrewd   dull, slow

**shatter**  break, fracture, crack, crush, split, smash, destroy

**shelter**  1. housing, quarters

**shelter**  2. protection, cover, refuge

**shield**  protect, defend, safeguard, cover, screen   expose

**shine**  glow, gleam, beam, sparkle, glimmer, glisten

**shiver**  shake, tremble, shudder, quiver

**shock**  startle, surprise, stun, jar

**shoot**  fire

**shop**  buy, purchase

**shore**  coast, beach, waterfront

**short**  1. little, small, puny   tall

**short**  2. brief, concise, succinct   long

**shortage**   lack, want, need, absence, deficiency   abundance

**shout**   scream, yell, howl, cry, call

**shove**   push, bump, nudge

**show**   1. demonstrate, illustrate, indicate, explain, clarify

**show**   2. performance, presentation, production, exhibit

**shrewd**   sharp, bright, clever, smart, alert, crafty, quick-witted, keen, sly   dull, slow

**shriek**   scream, yell, howl, cry, shout, screech, wail

**shrink**   become smaller, shrivel, wither   grow, expand

**shudder**   tremble, shake, shiver, quiver

**shuffle**   mix, scramble, jumble

**shut**   close, fasten, lock, seal   open

**shy**   bashful, timid, modest, coy   aggressive

**sick**   ill, ailing   well, healthy

**sight**   view, scene, vista, picture, spectacle

**sign**   1. endorse, write, mark

**sign**   2. signal, motion, gesture, indication

**silent**   quiet, still, hushed   noisy

**silly**   foolish, senseless, inane   sensible

**simple**   1. easy, clear, uncomplicated   difficult

**simple**   2. plain, ordinary

**sin**   evil, crime, offense

**sincere**   honest, truthful, genuine, unaffected   phony

**sing**   vocalize, chant

**singe**   sear, burn, scorch, char

**site**   place, location, area, spot, region

**situation**   case, condition, circumstance

**skillful**   handy, expert, clever, capable, apt, adept   awkward

**skimpy**   sparse, scanty, scarce   generous

**skinny**   thin, lean, scrawny, slim   chubby

**skip**   pass over, leave out, omit, miss, exclude   include

**slam**   close, bang, shut

**slant**   slope, tilt, incline

**slap**   hit, smack, strike

**slash**   slit, cut, sever, gash

**slavery**   captivity, bondage   freedom

**slay**   kill, murder, slaughter, exterminate, destroy

**sleep**   doze, nap, snooze, slumber

**slice**   cut, carve, slit

**slide**   glide, skid, slip

**sling**   splint, support, bandage

**slip**   1. slide, skid

**slip**   2. error, mistake, oversight, blunder

skinny

slide

**slit**  slash, cut, split, gash

**slope**  slant, incline, tilt

**sloppy**  careless, messy, untidy, slovenly  neat

**slow**  1. sluggish, delaying  fast

**slow**  2. dull, stupid, dim-witted  bright

**sly**  shrewd, sneaky, crafty, underhanded, shifty

**smack**  slap, hit, strike, crack, whack, wallop

**small**  little, slight, puny  big

**smart**  1. intelligent, bright, alert, wise, clever, quick
stupid

**smart**  2. pain, ache, hurt

**smash**  shatter, break, crack, split, destroy, demolish

smash

**smear**  1. smudge, soil, spot, stain

**smear**  2. spread, coat, dab

**smell**  scent, odor, aroma, fragrance

**smile**  grin, smirk  frown

**smog**  fog, haziness, cloudiness

**smooth**  polished, sleek, even  rough

**smother**  suffocate, muffle, stifle, choke

**smudge**  smear, soil, spot, stain

**snake**  serpent, viper

**snatch**  grab, seize, grasp, clutch  release

**snug**  cozy, comfortable, secure

soil (2)

**soak**   wet, drench, saturate  dry

**soap**   lather, shampoo

**sob**   cry, weep, bawl

**sociable**   friendly, cordial  unfriendly

**soft**   delicate, tender, fluffy, flexible  hard

**soggy**   damp, wet, moist, watery  dry

**soil**   1. dirty, spot, stain, smudge, smear

**soil**   2. ground, earth, dirt

**solemn**   sad, serious, grave, somber, grim, gloomy, glum  happy

**solid**   hard, firm, rigid, inflexible, sturdy, strong  soft, flimsy

**solution**   answer, explanation, finding, outcome, result

**solve**   answer, explain, figure out

**song**   tune, melody

**soon**   shortly, promptly, presently

**soothe**   calm, comfort, pacify

**sore**   painful, aching, tender

**sorrow**   sadness, grief, trouble, misfortune, suffering, misery  joy

**sorry**   apologetic, remorseful

**sort**   arrange, organize, classify, group, categorize

**sound**   noise

**souvenir**   remembrance, keepsake, memento, token

**spacious**   roomy, broad, vast   narrow

**spar**   box, fight

**sparkle**   shine, flash, glimmer, glitter, glisten, twinkle

**speak**   talk, comment

**special**   unusual, exceptional, notable, outstanding, extraordinary, remarkable   ordinary

**spectacular**   dramatic, sensational, marvelous, wonderful, extraordinary, glorious, great, grand, magnificent, splendid, superb, exciting, thrilling   ordinary, dull

**speedy**   fast, rapid, swift, quick, hasty

**spend**   pay out, use   save

**spice**   season, flavor

**spin**   turn, twirl, rotate, pivot

spin

**spirit**   courage, nerve, spunk

**spiteful**   mean, malicious, vindictive

**splendid**   glorious, great, grand, magnificent, superb, majestic, wonderful, divine, sensational, marvelous, fine, excellent

**split**   crack, break, separate, divide

**spoil**   1. damage, harm, hurt, destroy, ruin, upset, impair

**spoil**   2. rot, decay

**sponsor**   backer, supporter, promoter

spot (1)

**spook**  ghost, spirit, phantom

**spot**  1. soil, dirty, stain, smudge, smear

**spot**  2. pick out, recognize, identify, spy, sight, distinguish

**spread**  1. unfold, stretch out, sprawl

**spread**  2. distribute, scatter, disperse

**spry**  lively, active, energetic, spirited, agile, nimble  sluggish

**squad**  group, gang, crew

**squander**  waste, throw away  save

**squash**  crush, squeeze, mash

**squeeze**  press, pinch, crush

**squirt**  spurt, splash, spray, spout

**stab**  pierce, puncture, penetrate, perforate

**stack**  pile, heap, mound, load

**stage**  platform, podium

**stain**  dirty, spot, soil, smudge, smear, discolor

**stale**  old, spoiled  fresh

**stall**  delay, postpone, procrastinate

**stammer**  stutter, falter

**stamp**  1. seal, mark, label

**stamp**  2. pound, bang

**stampede**  rush, panic

**stand**  1. rise, get up

stage

**stand**  2. stay, remain, continue

**stand**  3. suffer, bear, tolerate

**stand**  4. base, pedestal

**stand**  5. booth, kiosk

**stanza**  verse, measure

**staple**  attach, fasten, join, connect

**star**  1. lead, headliner

**star**  2. heavenly body

**stare**  look, gaze, gape, gawk, glare

**start**  begin, commence, launch   end

**startle**  shock, surprise, stun, frighten, upset

**starvation**  hunger, famine

**state**  declare, say, exclaim, announce, tell, express, relate, report

**statement**  account, report, announcement, declaration

**station**  stop, depot

station

**stationary**  fixed, firm, immovable   movable

**stationery**  paper, writing materials

**statue**  figure, sculpture

**stay**  remain, continue, stand

**steady**  regular, constant, continuous   changing

**steal**  rob, take, burglarize

**steam**  vapor, gas, smoke

statue

105

**steer**  drive, handle, direct, manage, conduct, lead, head, command, run

**step**  walk, tread

**sterilize**  clean, sanitize, disinfect

**stern**  strict, harsh, rough, tough, hard, severe, firm  lenient, easygoing

**stick**  attach, adhere, cling

**stiff**  rigid, firm, unbending, hard, inflexible  flexible

**still**  quiet, calm, peaceful, serene, tranquil  noisy

**sting**  prick, wound

**stingy**  cheap, tight, miserly  generous

**stink**  smell, odor, stench

**stir**  mix, blend, combine, scramble

**stock**  supply, collection, reserve, inventory

**stomach**  belly, abdomen

**stone**  rock, pebble

stool

**stool**  seat, chair

**stop**  cease, end, halt, quit, conclude, discontinue  start

**store**  1. keep, stock, collect, save

**store**  2. shop, market

**storm**  gale, hurricane, tornado

**story**  tale, account, narrative

**stout**  fat, chubby, plump, stocky  thin

106

**strange**  odd, unusual, peculiar, queer, weird, bizarre
ordinary

**strangle**  choke, suffocate, smother

**stray**  wander, drift, roam, rove, meander

**stream**  creek, brook

**street**  road, avenue, thoroughfare

**strength**  power, force, might, energy, vigor
weakness

stream

**stretch**  extend, spread, expand

**strict**  stern, harsh, tough, exact, severe, firm   lenient

**strike**  hit, bat, slap, smack, slug, swat, knock

**strip**  remove, uncover, peel, bare   cover

**stripe**  line, mark, streak

**stroke**  rub, pet, pat, caress, fondle

**strong**  mighty, powerful, sturdy, hardy, tough,
healthy, rugged, robust, muscular   weak

**struggle**  battle, fight, feud, conflict

**stubborn**  obstinate, willful, headstrong, pigheaded,
ornery   flexible

**student**  pupil

**stuff**  fill, load, pack, cram   empty

**stumble**  trip, tumble, flounder, falter

**stun**  shock, startle, surprise, daze

**stunt**  feat, act, performance, exploit

**stupid**  dumb, dull, silly, foolish, dim-witted  smart

**stutter**  stammer, falter

**stylish**  fashionable, well-dressed  drab

**subject**  topic, issue, theme, question, point, plot

**substitute**  replace, change, exchange, trade, switch

**subtract**  deduct, remove, withdraw  add

**successful**  prosperous, well-off, fortunate, winning  unsuccessful

**sudden**  unexpected, abrupt, hasty

**sufficient**  enough, plenty, adequate  insufficient

**suffocate**  smother, stifle, choke

**suggestion**  proposal, plan, offer

**suitable**  proper, fitting, correct, appropriate  improper

**sum**  total, quantity

**summary**  review, outline, accounting

**sundown**  sunset, dusk, evening, nightfall  sunrise

**sunny**  bright, cheerful, pleasant  dull

**sunrise**  dawn, daybreak, morning  sunset

**sunset**  sundown, dusk, evening, nightfall  sunrise

**superb**  excellent, fine, splendid, glorious, great, grand, magnificent, wonderful, divine, sensational, marvelous

**supernatural**  ghostly, mystical

**supervise**   manage, direct, lead, guide, run, control, govern, command, head, boss

**supply**   provide, give, furnish

**support**   help, aid, assist, serve, encourage

**suppose**   believe, think, imagine, consider

**sure**   certain, positive, definite   uncertain

**surplus**   extra, additional, spare, leftover, excess   shortage

**surprise**   astonish, astound, amaze, startle, shock, stun

**surrender**   give up, quit, yield

**surround**   encircle, wrap

**survive**   live, remain, last

**suspect**   doubt, question, mistrust, distrust   trust

**suspense**   uncertainty, uneasiness, anxiety

**suspension**   1. removal, dismissal

**suspension**   2. interruption, break, pause, intermission

**swap**   trade, exchange, switch, barter

**swat**   hit, strike, smack, whack

**sway**   swing, rock, reel, swagger

**swear**   1. promise, vow, pledge, guarantee

**swear**   2. curse

**sweep**   clean, brush, vacuum

**sweet**   1. charming, lovely, pleasant, agreeable, adorable   disagreeable

swing

sword

**sweet**  2. sugary

**swift**  speedy, fast, rapid, quick, hasty  slow

**swindle**  cheat, trick, defraud, bamboozle

**swing**  sway, rock, hang, dangle

**switch**  change, exchange, swap, trade, substitute

**sword**  knife, blade

**symbol**  token, emblem

**sympathy**  understanding, pity, compassion

**symptom**  sign, mark, indication

**system**  method, plan, manner, means, way, style,
  procedure

# T

**tactful**  thoughtful, considerate, kind, sensitive, diplo-
  matic  tactless

**tag**  1. follow, shadow, trail, pursue, tail

**tag**  2. label, name, brand

**tail**  1. follow, shadow, trail, pursue, tag

**tail**  2. back, rear, end

**take** 1. seize, capture, get, obtain   give

**take** 2. carry, bring, transport

**tale** story, account

**talent** ability, skill, know-how, gift, forte

**talk** speak, discuss, converse

**tall** 1. big, large   short

**tall** 2. high, lofty   small

**tame** gentle, obedient, mild, domesticated   wild

**tangle** twist, knot, snarl

**tantrum** fit, outburst, flare-up

**tap** 1. rap, pat

**tap** 2. faucet, spigot

tap (2)

**tape** 1. wrap, bind, tie

**tape** 2. record

**target** aim, goal, object, purpose

**tart** sour, sharp, bitter, pungent   sweet

**task** chore, job, work, assignment, duty

**taste** sample, test, try, savor

**tavern** inn, bar, saloon, pub

**tax** duty, toll, tariff

**taxi** cab, hack

taxi

**teach** instruct, show, educate, inform, tell, advise, tutor

**111**

**team**   gang, group, crew, band

**tear**   rip, cut, split, slit, slash

**tease**   annoy, bother, pester, badger, provoke

**televise**   telecast, broadcast

**tell**   relate, recite, narrate, report, state, explain, inform, convey

**temperamental**   moody, sensitive, touchy

**temporary**   passing, momentary, short-lived, transient
permanent

**tenant**   occupant, resident

**tense**   nervous, anxious, strained, uptight, rigid
relaxed

**term**   period, time, duration

**terrible**   horrible, horrid, dreadful, awful, atrocious
wonderful

**terrific**   marvelous, wonderful, glorious, great, magnificent, splendid, superb, sensational   ordinary

**terrify**   frighten, scare, alarm, horrify, shock, petrify

**territory**   region, district, area, section, zone

**test**   1. examine, question, quiz

**test**   2. try, sample, experiment, attempt

**thankful**   grateful, appreciative

**thaw**   melt, defrost

**theater**   playhouse, hall

theater

**thick**  broad, bulky, solid  thin

**thief**  robber, burglar, crook

**thin**  skinny, lean, slim, slender  fat

**think**  1. believe, suppose, imagine, expect, guess, suspect, assume

**think**  2. consider, reflect, ponder

**thirsty**  dry, parched, dehydrated

**thorough**  complete, all-out, intensive  incomplete

**thought**  1. idea, notion, concept

**thought**  2. care, attention, regard, concern

**thoughtful**  considerate, kind, sympathetic  thoughtless

**thoughtless**  inconsiderate, unkind  thoughtful

**threaten**  warn, bully, intimidate, bulldoze, terrorize, harass

**thrifty**  economical, careful, frugal  wasteful

**thrilling**  exciting, delightful, enchanting, stirring, moving, breathtaking  boring

**throw**  pitch, toss, fling, hurl, cast

**ticket**  1. pass, voucher

**ticket**  2. summons, subpoena, citation

**tidy**  neat, orderly, well-kept, trim  sloppy

**tie**  fasten, secure, bind, wrap  untie

**tight**  snug, firm  loose

throw

**tilt**   slope, slant, incline

**timid**   shy, bashful, reserved, meek   bold

**tint**   color, dye, stain

**tiny**   little, small, minute, puny   huge

**tip**   1. end, point, extremity

**tip**   2. gratuity, bonus

**tip**   3. advice, information, clue

**tired**   exhausted, weary, fatigued   rested

**title**   name, heading

**toll**   charge, fee, fare

**tone**   sound, pitch, key

**tool**   instrument, device, implement, utensil, gadget

**top**   head, peak, tip, summit   bottom

**topic**   subject, issue, theme, question, point

**topple**   fall, drop, tumble, collapse

**torch**   light, lantern

**tornado**   windstorm, tempest

**torture**   agony, pain, torment

**toss**   throw, pitch, fling, hurl, cast

**total**   1. whole, entire, complete   partial

**total**   2. add, sum up, count

**touch**   feel, handle, contact

**tough**   1. hardy, strong, sturdy, rugged, robust   weak

torch

tornado

114

**tough**  2. hard, difficult, rough, complicated  easy
**tour**  trip, excursion, journey
**tournament**  contest, game, match, competition
**tow**  pull, haul, drag, tug
**toxic**  poisonous, deadly, venomous
**trace**  copy, reproduce, duplicate, outline
**track**  path, trail, road, course
**trade**  1. exchange, barter, switch, swap, bargain
**trade**  2. business, work, line, employment
**tradition**  custom, habit
**tragic**  sad, disastrous, unfortunate, dreadful
**trail**  1. follow, chase, tail, track, pursue
**trail**  2. track, path, road, course
**train**  1. teach, drill, practice, exercise, prepare, condition, groom

**train**  2. railroad cars

train (2)

**traitor**  betrayer, spy, informer
**tramp**  vagrant, hobo, vagabond
**transfer**  hand over, deliver, pass, change
**translate**  interpret
**trap**  catch, capture, seize, hook, snare  release
**trash**  rubbish, waste, garbage, refuse, scrap, junk, litter, debris
**travel**  journey, tour

**treasure**   1. adore, idolize, cherish, appreciate, value

**treasure**   2. fortune, wealth, riches

**treat**   1. deal with, handle, regard, tend to

**treat**   2. delight, pleasure, thrill

**treaty**   pact, agreement, understanding, alliance

**tremble**   shake, shudder, quiver

**tremendous**   gigantic, colossal, huge, giant, vast, enormous, immense   tiny

**trial**   1. test, experiment, tryout

**trial**   2. court case

**tribe**   group, clan, sect

**trick**   deceive, mislead, fool, dupe

**trim**   1. cut, shave, pare

**trim**   2. decorate, beautify, adorn

**trip**   1. stumble, tumble, fall, falter

**trip**   2. tour, journey, excursion

**troop**   group, company, squad, unit

**trophy**   award, prize, reward

**trouble**   bother, difficulty, inconvenience

**truant**   absentee

**truce**   armistice

**true**   genuine, real, pure, authentic, actual, valid, right, proper, correct, accurate, exact   false

**trust**   believe, accept   distrust

trophy

**try**   test, sample, experiment, attempt
**tug**   pull, tow, drag, yank, haul
**tumble**   fall, topple, drop
**tune**   melody, song
**tunnel**   passage, channel
**turn**   rotate, spin, swivel, pivot, twist
**tutor**   teach, instruct, coach
**twinkle**   sparkle, shine, glimmer, glitter, glisten, gleam
**twirl**   turn, spin, twist, whirl
**twist**   turn, twirl, spin
**twitch**   jerk, shudder, spasm
**type**   kind, sort, variety, class, category, group, species
**tyrant**   dictator, taskmaster, slave driver

tumble

# U

umpire

**ugly**   homely, unattractive, hideous   beautiful
**umpire**   referee, judge, mediator
**unable**   unfit, incapable, powerless   able
**unanimous**   agreed, in accord, harmonious
**unaware**   ignorant, unknowing   aware

**unbelievable** 1. incredible, absurd, fantastic

**unbelievable** 2. doubtful, questionable, suspicious
believable

**uncertain** doubtful, unsure, undecided, unpredictable
certain

**unchanged** same, steady, constant changed

**uncivilized** savage, wild, unrefined civilized

**uncomfortable** awkward, cramped, unpleasant
comfortable

**uncommon** unusual, rare, scarce, unique, different,
novel, original common

**unconscious** out cold, senseless, comatose
conscious

**unconstitutional** unlawful, illegal legal

**uncover** reveal, show, expose, disclose cover,
conceal

**undecided** uncertain, doubtful, unsure, indefinite,
vague certain

**under** below, beneath above, over

**understand** follow, see, know, appreciate, grasp,
comprehend

**undress** unclothe, disrobe, strip dress

**unemployed** jobless, idle, unoccupied employed

**unexpected** sudden, unforeseen, unplanned
expected

**unfair**   unjust, partial   fair

**unfaithful**   untrue, disloyal, fickle   faithful

**unfamiliar**   strange, unusual, new, different
   familiar

**unfortunate**   unlucky, sad, unhappy   fortunate

**unfriendly**   antisocial, cool, distant, aloof   friendly

**ungrateful**   unappreciative, thankless   grateful

**unhappy**   sad, depressed, dejected, downhearted, blue,
   sorrowful, downcast, gloomy, glum, forlorn, melan-
   choly   happy

unhappy

**unhealthy**   sickly, ill, ailing, frail, weak   healthy

**uniform**   outfit, costume

**unimportant**   petty, minor, trivial, insignificant
   important

**unnecessary**   needless, useless, uncalled-for
   necessary

**unoccupied**   vacant, available, open, empty   occupied

**unpack**   unload, empty   pack

**unpleasant**   nasty, disagreeable, unlikable, offensive,
   obnoxious   pleasant

**unpopular**   disliked, unwanted   popular

**unreasonable**   ridiculous,   absurd,   extreme
   reasonable

**unruly**   disorderly, wild, disobedient   orderly

**unsafe**  dangerous, risky, hazardous  safe

**unsatisfactory**  poor, inferior, second-rate, inadequate  satisfactory

**unsuccessful**  failing, unfortunate  successful

**untie**  loosen, undo, unfasten  tie

**unusual**  uncommon, rare, unique, different, novel, original  usual

**unwilling**  opposed, reluctant  willing

**uphold**  support, maintain, defend, back

**upright**  1. standing, erect, vertical

**upright**  2. honorable, respectable, moral

**uprising**  revolution, revolt, riot, rebellion

**uproar**  noise, racket, clamor, commotion, disturbance, tumult, hubbub  peace

**upset**  disturb, annoy, bother, unnerve  soothe

**urge**  push, press, advise, prod, coax, prompt  discourage

**urgent**  necessary, important, essential, vital, crucial  unimportant

**useful**  helpful, practical, handy, valuable, beneficial  useless

**useless**  worthless  useful

**usher**  guide, escort

**usual**  common, regular, normal, ordinary, familiar, everyday, typical  unusual

usher

120

# V

**vacant** unoccupied, available, open, empty filled, occupied

**vacation** leave, break, recess, holiday

**valuable** important, significant, precious, costly, expensive

**value** worth, cost

**vandalism** destruction, ruination

**vanish** disappear, fade appear

**vapor** steam, fog, mist

**various** several, different, many, numerous, assorted

**vary** change, alter

**vast** huge, immense, enormous, great tiny

**vegetation** plants, growth, flora

**verdict** decision, ruling, finding, judgment

**verse** 1. poetry, rhyme

**verse** 2. passage, section, part, division

**version** account, story, description, interpretation

**veto** refuse, deny approve

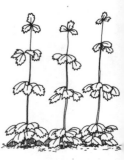

vegetation

**vibrate**   shake, quiver

**vicious**   ferocious, fierce, savage, brutal, cruel, ruthless, evil, wicked, mean

**victim**   loser, underdog, sufferer, prey

**victory**   triumph, success, winning   defeat

**view**   sight, scene, vista, picture

**villain**   scoundrel, rascal, devil

**violate**   break, disobey

**violence**   rage, anger, frenzy, fury

**vision**   1. eyesight, perception

**vision**   2. image, illusion, fantasy, dream

**volunteer**   offer, come forward

**vote**   ballot, choice, selection

**voyage**   journey, cruise, crossing

# W

wake

**wag**   wave, flap, swing, shake

**wake**   get up, arise

**walk**   stroll

**wallop**   smack, slap, hit, strike, crack, whack, thrash, beat, slug

122

**wander**   stray, drift, roam, rove, ramble

**want**   desire, wish for, long for, crave

**war**   battle, fight, feud, struggle, combat, conflict

**warn**   1. caution, inform, notify, alert

**warn**   2. threaten

**wash**   launder, clean, scrub

**waste**   squander, misuse  save

wash

**watch**   1. observe, see, look at

**watch**   2. guard, protect, defend, shield

**wave**   sway, move, flap

**wax**   polish, shine, glaze

**weak**   feeble, frail, powerless  strong

**wealthy**   rich, comfortable, well-to-do, affluent, prosperous  poor

**wed**   marry, join, unite

**weird**   queer, odd, strange, peculiar, unusual, creepy, spooky, eerie  normal

**welcome**   greet, receive

wed

**whack**   wallop, smack, slap, hit, strike, crack, thrash, beat, slug

**whip**   strike, beat, thrash, flog, crack

**whole**   complete, total, entire  partial

**wicked**   evil, bad, sinful, mean, cruel, ruthless, vicious  good, saintly

**wide**   broad, expansive  narrow

123

win

**wife**  spouse, mate, married woman

**wig**  hairpiece

**wild**  1. untamed, uncivilized, savage, ferocious  civilized, tame

**wild**  2. reckless, rash, crazy, frenzied  calm

**willing**  agreeable, ready, consenting  unwilling

**win**  succeed, triumph, prevail  lose

**1. wind**  air, breeze, gust

**2. wind**  turn, twist, coil

**wire**  telegraph, cable

**wise**  smart, intelligent, clever, knowledgeable, learned, educated, scholarly  uneducated

**wish**  desire, long for, want, crave

**withdraw**  remove, subtract, deduct  deposit

**without**  lacking, wanting, needing, missing, minus, less  with

**witty**  clever, amusing, funny, humorous

**wonderful**  marvelous, glorious, great, grand, magnificent, splendid, superb, divine, sensational, spectacular  horrible

**woods**  forest

**work**  1. labor, toil

**work**  2. operate, run, manage, handle

**workout**  exercise, practice, drill

124

**world**   universe, earth

**worn**   used, old, secondhand, ragged   new

**worried**   troubled, concerned, disturbed, upset, nervous   calm

**worship**   adore, idolize, cherish, revere

**wound**   injury, hurt, bruise

**wrap**   cover, bind, tie   uncover

**wreath**   garland

**wreck**   destroy, ruin, demolish

**wring**   squeeze, twist

**wrong**   incorrect, inaccurate, faulty, mistaken   right

wreath

# X

**x-ray**   picture, photograph

# Y

**yacht**   boat

yacht

yarn

**yank**  pull, tug, jerk
**yarn**  wool, thread
**yell**  shout, scream, howl, cry, call, shriek, screech
**yield**  1. produce, give, provide, supply
**yield**  2. surrender, give up, sacrifice
**young**  youthful, juvenile  old
**youngster**  child, minor, youth, kid

# Z

**zero**  nothing, nil, none
**zone**  region, district, area, section, territory
**zoo**  menagerie
**zoom**  speed, zip, whiz, fly